Commodification
and Spectacle
in Architecture

Harvard Design Magazine Readers
William S. Saunders, Editor

Commodification and Spectacle in Architecture

A Harvard Design Magazine Reader

Introduction by Kenneth Frampton

William S. Saunders, Editor

University of Minnesota Press | Minneapolis | London

These essays were previously published in *Harvard Design Magazine*, Harvard University Graduate School of Design; Peter G. Rowe, Dean, 1992–2004; Alan Altshuler, Dean, 2005–.

Special thanks to Graham Gund of Graham Gund Architects, Cambridge, Massachusetts, for financial support for the commission of the Introduction to this book. Thanks also to coordinator Meghan Ryan for her work on *Harvard Design Magazine*.

Published by the University of Minnesota Press
111 Third Avenue South, Suite 290
Minneapolis, MN 55401-2520
http://www.upress.umn.edu

Library of Congress Cataloging-in-Publication Data

    Commodification and spectacle in architecture : a Harvard Design Magazine reader / introduction by Kenneth Frampton ; William S. Saunders, editor.
       p.   cm. — (Harvard Design Magazine readers ; 1)
    ISBN 0-8166-4752-6 (hc : alk. paper) — ISBN 0-8166-4753-4 (pb : alk. paper)
    1. Architecture and society. 2. Architecture—Economic aspects.
  3. Architecture and globalization. 4. Architecture, Postmodern.
  I. Saunders, William S. II. Series.
    NA2543.S6C66 2005
    720'.1'03—dc22
                                     2005021172

Printed in the United States of America on acid-free paper

The University of Minnesota is an equal-opportunity educator and employer.

12 11 10 09 08 07 06 05   10 9 8 7 6 5 4 3 2 1

Contents

Preface

William S. Saunders

This book is the first in a series addressing urgent contemporary issues in design and the built environment. The diverse and often conflicting points of view presented in these essays will allow readers to understand the significant concerns and points of debate. The assumption is not that all positions articulated here are equally "right," but that one needs to understand the ways in which reasonable people can disagree to clarify one's own thinking about these issues.

These essays were selected from the pages of *Harvard Design Magazine: Architecture, Landscape Architecture, Urban Design and Planning*, from issues from 1998 to 2004. That writers have returned to the themes of commodification and spectacle during seven years is an indication of their persistence and urgency.

What then are the issues, realities, and problems encompassed by the terms *commodification* and *spectacle*? Any summary will simplify, but the broad strokes are these: along with every other cultural production (including music, photography, book publishing, the fine arts, and even education), the design of the built environment has been increasingly engulfed in and made subservient to the goals of the capitalist economy, more specifically the luring of consumers for the purpose of gaining their money. Design is more than ever a means to an extrinsic end rather than an end in itself.

A telling example is the Frank Gehry–designed Guggenheim Museum in Bilbao, Spain. However wonderful and even "great" this building may be as a "purely" architectural presence, it simply cannot be thought of apart from its intended role in promoting the economic revitalization of Bilbao and its magnetic power for tourist money.

Spectacle is the primary manifestation of the commodification or commercialization of design: design that is intended to seduce consumers will likely be more or less spectacular, more or less a matter of flashy, stimulating, quickly experienced gratification, more or less essentially like a television ad. The stimulation that leads to "Wow!" or to immediate sensual pleasure is more prominent than any implicit invitation to slow savoring and reflection. When the *making* of spectacles—like special effects in movies—is imagined and understood, they collapse, deflated. When the making of a more "disinterested" cultural phenomenon (Louis Kahn's Kimball Museum, for instance) is imagined, it expands in interest. While spectacle discourages independent thought, "art" depends on it.

At the same time, writers in this volume actively reject any dreamy nostalgia that would idealize present or past "art" as ever completely devoid of seductive motives and a role in the marketplace. The Medicis may have commissioned "fine art," but that art served a role in their establishment of status and power.

The central debate among writers about the commodification of architecture and other environmental arts is whether and to what extent it is possible for designers to resist, escape, or offer substantial alternatives to the dominant commercial culture. Curiously, the Marxist tradition leads both to a sense that culture is inevitably determined by its economic base and to leftist rebellion against the powers that be. In this book, believers in resistance (Michael Sorkin, Rick Poynor, and Thomas Frank, as well as Kenneth Frampton in his introduction) predominate. But among those who reject resistance as naive, dreamy, or moralistic, a new note is struck: what is so bad about commercial culture? Its many pleasures are harmless.

I would imagine that readers will be asking, most of all, just how harmless or harmful contemporary commodification and spectacle are.

Introduction
The Work of Architecture in the Age of Commodification
Kenneth Frampton

Over the past three decades international monopoly capital has increasingly challenged the authority of the nation-state, which still ostensibly embodies the democratic precepts of the free world. In this weakening of sovereignty, dating back to the revocation of the postwar Bretton Woods agreement, we have reason to believe that the last politically independent nation-state will be France, for France remains a state where the public intellectual plays a part in the country's political life. It is this perhaps that accounts for the apocalyptic tone of French sociopolitical analysis. I have in mind the long haul that runs from Henri Lefebvre's *The Survival of Capitalism* (1973) to Michel Houellebecq's recent dystopic vision of a society of "isolated individuals pursuing independent aims of mutual indifference," as paraphrased by Luis Fernández-Galiano in his essay "Spectacle and Its Discontents; or, The Elusive Joys of Architainment." I open with the theme of the public intellectual because with the exceptions of Fernández-Galiano, Thomas Frank, Rick Poynor, and Michael Sorkin, most of the authors represented in this anthology tend to evade the psychopolitical substrate underlying the compulsions of our commodified society. It is as though they would prefer to avoid a critical confrontation with socioeconomic causes that are directly responsible for the environmental degradation of the late modern world.

Despite more than half a century of psychosociological research, the formation of identity at both an individual and a group level, along with the artificial stimulation of desire, jointly remains among the more opaque aspects of Anglo-American culture, particularly in view of the disturbing fact that in the 2000 presidential election fewer than half of eligible U.S. voters actually voted and that a large number of those who did vote then and in 2004 gave their support to candidates whose policies run counter to their class interests. While hints of this depoliticized malaise are latent in almost every contribution to this volume, there is nonetheless a tendency to avoid any reference to the benighted socialist alternative, as though this political option is so discredited by history and the triumph of the market as to be irrelevant.

This is at once evident in Michael Benedikt's essay "Less for Less Yet," which affords the reader a rigorous analysis of some of the aporia surrounding the profession, beginning with the wholesale commodification of the environment, although Benedikt elects to shift the blame for this regrettable condition to the supposedly self-inflected marginality of the architectural profession, which, as is commonly known, is responsible for the design of only 2 percent of the annual built production, rather than to accord some of this responsibility to the manipulated consensus politics of the two-party system, locked in a perennial struggle to gain the decisive 5 percent of the vote that will ease one party or the other into power—that is to say, politics for the sake of getting elected as opposed to a politic dedicated to the welfare of the society. Benedikt's skepticism renders him only too ready to accept the populist adage that people vote with their wallets instead of their ballots, provided that they are fortunate enough to have sufficient disposable income. Thus we are informed, in Benedikt's exceptionally trenchant manner,

> In societies at peace that can maintain free markets, people can get what they want; what they want depends on how successfully their needs and values are addressed by competing producers. With a modicum of prosperity, people have choices. This is the context in which architecture, as an industry, broadly conceived, has become less and less able to deliver a superior, evolving, and popularly engaging product that can compete with other, more successful products— with cars, music, movies, sports, and travel, to name a few. And the less successfully architecture has competed with these diverse "growth industries," the less architects have been entrusted with time

and money to perform work on a scale and with a quality that could, perhaps, turn things around.

While one may readily share Benedikt's critique of the irrelevance of elitist aestheticism and his parallel impatience with the reductive maximization of digital design and with the more arcane aspects of contemporary architectural theory, one can hardly be sanguine about his economic determinism rendered exclusively in terms of populist market forces. It is somehow unconscionable, given his realistic stance, that he has nothing to say about the not-so-benign neglect of public transport in the United States or about the concomitant barely hidden subsidization of the automobile through various stratagems, from the federally subsidized interstate system to the proliferation of urban sprawl first, in the postwar era, through the FHA mortgage regulations and subsequently through the combination of land-use ordinances and local building codes, both of which have paradoxically encouraged the continual subdivision of agricultural land. As architect turned "free-marketer," Benedikt seemingly would prefer not to concern himself with such phenomena as the still-expanding urbanized regions of the United States that so far planners have been unable to check due to the stranglehold that private land-holding interests exercise over contemporary development. It says something for the "newspeak" of our time that Benedikt feels that he may legitimately refer to architecture as an industry as opposed to a liberal profession. His thesis is that architecture could be restructured as a "growth industry" and thereby respond to the popular taste of the free market, although what he has in mind when he speaks of being able "to turn things around" is far from clear.

One is inclined to be more sympathetic to the critical tone of the Benedikt contribution than to the letter of its populist rhetoric, for if there is one thing that perennially escapes our professional attention—above all the attention of contemporary architectural educators—it is the need to devise a sustainable and simultaneously socially accessible middle-class land settlement pattern for future residential development. Since Serge Chermayeff and Christopher Alexander's *Community and Privacy* (1963), hardly anyone in the field has bothered to scratch the surface of this problem, and yet, at many levels, it remains the most fundamental environmental challenge of our time.

It would be hard to find a more passionate advocate of design marketing than Kevin Ervin Kelley, who, in his worldly essay "Architecture for Sale(s)," boldly demonstrates how this may be best achieved as a comprehensive service by suppressing the term *architecture* altogether.

> Calling what our firm does "architecture" was quite confusing for all involved, so we redefined our service as "Perception Design"—we help prompt consumers to buy through environmental "signaling" that influences their perceptions. In a sense, we are designing the consumers themselves. Brand cueing takes place in the built elements but also the menu, uniforms, logo, aromas, and music, plus sensations, and, most importantly, emotions. Most architects are surprised that our firm generally will not take on a project unless we are involved in evaluating all elements of the brand. We changed the firm's name to the single word *Shook* with the tag line "It's All Consuming." We thus tell people that we eagerly embrace consumerism.

Although Peter Behrens was one of the world's first "house designers" when he became the architect to the AEG corporation in 1908, he would have hardly understood the demagogic ephemeral nature of *branding* in today's terms. At the turn of the century, Behrens could still entertain the illusion that he was determining the overall quality of a new industrial civilization, whereas today's brand designers are dedicated not only to the gratification of consumer taste but also to the stimulation of desire, knowing full well that everything depends on the sublimating eroticism of consumption as opposed to the intrinsic quality of the thing consumed. As Kelley puts it: "People *enjoy* the experience of buying, sometimes more than having the products themselves, because the moment of buying is one of enthusiastic fantasy and escape."

Nothing could be further from Kelley's Candide-like euphoria than Michael Sorkin's essay "Brand Aid" through which, as in several other essays in this book, the figure of Rem Koolhaas stalks like a cultural shade. Sorkin is hyperaware of this ideological nemesis at every step, above all in his sardonic assessment of the 1998 Guggenheim motorcycle show, sponsored by BMW and designed by Frank Gehry, of which he writes:

> The match of Rem and Krens— two tall men with flat affects— is a great one: both are selling the same product: products. "Shopping is arguably the last remaining form of public activity," opines Koolhaas. And so we shop for Picassos and Kandinskys, for Harleys and Yamahas, for Prada shoes and Bulgari brooches, all under the

aura of the covetable pots of gold at the end of the fleeting rainbows glistening about the roulette tables and the high-stakes slots. Just as the way out of the museum leads through the shop, the exit from the casino is lined with boutiques and museums. At the motorcycle exhibition, the stairway is painted in Prada's signature chartreuse to reinforce the point. The retina is the point of sale: to see is to buy. In contemporary "casino capitalism," citizenship is a credit line, democracy a crapshoot.

For very different reasons, Sorkin follows Kelley and the versatile critic Thomas Frank in recognizing that ultimately the brand is not something fixed like a universal logo but rather something elusive, such as a mood or a desire, in a constant state of evocative formulation. As Frank puts it, quoting a British pamphlet introducing account planning, "Advertising is a means of contributing meaning and values that are necessary and useful to people in structuring their lives, their casual relationships, and their rituals." Frank's somewhat ambivalent assessment of the role of advertising in relation to democracy is quite removed from Kelley's enthusiastic acclaim of branding as a means of conferring on a political candidate the deceptive aura of *trust* that will help to ensure his or her election.

Sorkin touches on similar disconcerting convergences when he remarks on the parallel, paradoxical interdependence between late capitalism and contemporary art and on the way in which this mutual dependency possesses equally sobering ramifications for architecture. Thus we read:

> Just as Koolhaas promotes his own brand with a blizzard of statistics, photos of the "real" world, and a weary sense of globalism's inescapable surfeit and waste as the only legitimate field of architectural action, the New Urbanists—with their own megalomaniac formulas of uniformity—create their slightly "different" Vegas of "traditional" architecture based on its association with the imagined reality of bygone happinesses. Their tunes may differ, but both are lyricists for the ideological master narrative that validates and celebrates the imperial machine.

From which we may understand that in different ways architecture has become a brand in itself, particularly for the "signature" architect, whose mediatic overvaluation finds a direct correspondence in the systematic undervaluation of other equally if not more talented architects whose work has yet to be confirmed by the mediatic consensus as a discernable and desirable brand.

Sorkin is at pains to point out that the brand syndrome also operates at another more surreptitious level than the upfront mediatic promotion of star architects. This is the implicit corporate brand whereby, copying the acronymic formulation of SOM, architectural offices assert their corporate status by adopting logolike initials such as KPF, HOK, NBBJ, and even OMA, with which Koolhaas has promoted his own international operation. In this subliminal sleight of hand, the delirious neo-avant-garde enlarges its scope through assuming the aura of corporate power.

Koolhaas's ambivalence about the value of architecture in the late modern world has been rarely so forcefully characterized as in Wouter Vanstiphout's dichotomous appraisal in "Rockbottom" of the chasm that divides Koolhaas's dystopic diagnosis from his programmatic, cinematically indulgent practice as an architect. Thus, while being only too appreciative of Koolhaas's spectacular house for a paraplegic publisher near Bordeaux, complete with its extralarge hydraulic elevator, Vanstiphout loses his patience with Rem's invidious comparisons between the hyperproduction of China's building industry and the diminutive output of contemporary occidental architects. He vents his spleen with Rem's ambivalent public posture with a rhetorical question:

> Why does he sardonically state that in China architects produce ten times as much, ten times as fast and do it ten times as cheaply as their European counterparts and therefore can be said to be a thousand times as good, and say this at the opening of an exhibition of projects that have taken an ungodly amount of design time, for small fees, only to make something desperately unique, utterly authentic, personal, and seriously Architectural?

In "Hyphenation Nation," Rick Poynor draws our attention to the received contemporary wisdom that *hybridity* is the inescapable destiny of postmodern environmental culture, from the works of charismatic star architects to the processes of multinational, corporate design practices. Inspired by the socioeconomic prognostications of the Swedish business gurus Jonas Ridderstråle and Kjell Nordström, Poynor argues that maximization of profit in contemporary society depends on a categorical departure from any kind of traditional division of labor, be this in commerce, education, or many other diverse under-

takings. By their endorsement of such expressions as *infotainment,
distance learning, bio-tech,* and *corporate university*—all of which are
symptomatic of what these hipster Swedes call new wealth-generating
bundles—one comes to realize that Fernández-Galiano's coinage of
the term *architainment* is only too prescient. Beyond being merely an
acerbic comment, this term may be viewed as the touchstone of a new
way of "making it," as Will Alsop's brashly irresponsible yet highly
successful practice surely serves to confirm.

The fact is that, as Poynor remarks, the arts of visual communication, as opposed to architecture, have long since been co-opted by the
admass drives of the advertising industry, which from its inception has
harnessed graphic and filmic expression to its own rhetorical ends, as
we may appreciate from the work of such a renowned pioneering
graphist as Lucien Bernhard, not to mention the more comprehensive
hybrid practices of our own time such as Bruce Mau's *Life Style* in
his celebrated book of that title, wherein he searches somewhat dif-
fidently for an exit from the closed consumerist circuit of our time, or
of the late Tibor Kalman, who worked for Benetton while naively be-
lieving that one could still "find the cracks in the wall" through which
one could escape from the consumerist dead end of international monopoly capital. Not since the welfare state socialism of the interwar
and postwar periods in the first half of the twentieth century has it
been possible to employ visual communication over a broad front for
purposes other than advertising products.

Poynor makes us acutely aware of this by drawing attention to
the now forty-year-old graphic design manifesto *First Things First,*
reworked in the year 2000 in time for the antiglobalization protests
staged at the WTO meeting in Seattle in that year. That this manifesto, drafted by socially conscious graphic designers, was rejected
out of hand by the "rank and file" of the design profession is hardly
surprising. A similar *rappel à l'ordre* written by a minority of politically engaged architects and addressed to the profession at large
would almost certainly be equally ill received. The capacity of architects and their apologists to accept the trivialization of the field in the
late modern world through the reduction of everything to representation and/or misrepresentation seems to be enthusiastically entertained
by Daniel Naegele's warm appraisal in "We Dig Graves—All Sizes"
of the spectacular industrial design activity of Michael Graves. Unlike
the misgivings entertained by Mau and Kalman and even Koolhaas
when he argues that "not shopping" is the only luxury left in the late

modern world, Naegele remains totally sanguine about Graves's infantilized Disneyfication of everyday domestic objects.

Thomas Frank's essay "Rocking for the Clampdown" enters the list at this point by suggesting that there may be more than a casual link between the tortuously innovative accounting of the New Economy and Frank Gehry's cacophonic rendering of Paul Allen's Experience Music Project in Seattle. He reminds us early on of Enron's patronage of the 2002 Frank Gehry retrospective at the Guggenheim Museum and of the fact that the foreword to the catalog for the show was written by none other than Jeffrey Skilling at the very moment when he was already under investigation. As Skilling put it, "This is the search Enron embarks on every day, by questioning the conventional to change business paradigms and create new markets that will shape the New Economy. It is the shared sense of challenge that we admire most in Frank Gehry, and we hope that this exhibition will bring you as much inspiration as it has brought us."

In a remarkably subtle excursus, Frank sets forth the sociocultural-cum-economic vectors that have interacted in the rock music industry over the past forty years to forge a surprising link between the counterculture of the 1960s—embodied in the music of Jimi Hendrix—and the politically reactionary conservatism of the United States that served as the paradoxical proving ground for the new digital economy. To much the same end, Paul Allen's cybernetically contrived reenactment of rock culture depends on interactive feedback loops and simulated "play alongs" by virtue of which the visitor may vicariously reexperience the music of an epoch. All these populist, hypothetically democratic "samplings" would perhaps entail some radical conviction were it not for the fact that, as Frank unsparingly observes,

> Today we know enough about Allen's Microsoft to understand that temp agencies do not empower workers, that the reign of "interactivity" permitted monopolies with unprecedented power, that popular participation in stock markets allowed a concentration of wealth that we had not seen since the 1920s. In this sense "interactivity" was an ideological smokescreen, a democratic, do-it-yourself myth that concealed the fantastic growth of autocratic corporate power.

In this context, as Frank remarks, there is an odd but symptomatic disjunction between the blue, red, and gold mirage of Gehry's exterior, supposedly representing a smashed guitar (a figure perceivable, as Hal Foster has suggested, only from the air or the top of Seattle's space needle) and the ad hoc, banged together, backstage character of the interior. Is it possible to see this contrast as testifying to the split between the neon-lit facade of the Silicon Valley bubble and the loosely "wired" house of cards that lay just beneath its surface? Paul Allen's somewhat sardonic gesture of smashing a glass guitar at the opening of his $240-million nostalgic folly was presumably a public reenactment of the efficacy of an orgiastic destruction as the guarantor of worldly success. As Frank proceeds to point out, this corporate article of faith in hyper-innovation has become somewhat tainted of late by the inequity of insider trading, excessive stock options, and all the conveniently ingenious accounting methods that have since become a synonym for fraud.

Where is the anachronistic culture of architecture to situate itself in the face of all this digitally dematerialized representation and misrepresentation? In formulating such a rhetorical question, I am, I suppose, harking back to Frank Lloyd Wright's paradoxically creative evocation of the "cause conservative" as a hypothetically progressive principle. This is at least one way of asking the question as to what we might mean, in this fungible age, by such terms as *sustainable environmental design* or, let us say, even *tradition,* in as much as the finest work of any epoch always amounts to a critical reinterpretation of tradition. Of course nothing could be further from this than the maximization of innovation as an end in itself or the romantic cult of destruction and waste as a kind of latter-day capitalist potlatch. As Adolf Loos put it, with his characteristic irony, "There is no point in inventing anything unless it is an improvement." To put it more evenhandedly, in what way may we modulate some future possible relationship between creativity and homeostasis or, let us say, between human imaginative capacity and the now all-too-evident limitations of the biosphere? This is surely the one question that the contemporary cult of the populist free market is unable to address. By and large today's realistic critical opinion, as a number of these essays suggest, prefers to focus on the de facto consumerist gratification of engineered desire as a contemporary delirium rather than to dwell on the ongoing and pervasive corruption of democratic culture through the agency of the mass media.

How one may offset this globalized closure becomes a question not only for architectural practice but also for all the multifarious schools of architecture and urbanism. At this juncture one can hardly emphasize enough how the substance of political process needs to be articulated within the field, both pedagogically and otherwise, not only in relation to the big politics of large-scale environmental policy, to be argued for agonistically in the public realm, but also in the small politics of psychosocial well-being and sustainability, as these factors may be incorporated at a microscale into environmental design. On the one hand, then, political consciousness, in the broadest sense, ought to be as much part of design education as any other component in an architectural curriculum; on the other hand, it is necessary to maintain an ethical dimension in the culture of design itself. This last surely corresponds to that which Morris Berman in his book *The Twilight of American Culture* has called "the monastic option." It is this that is implicitly advanced by Poynor as a strategy by which to transcend the spectacle of neo-avant-gardist kitsch (quasi-radical in form but nihilistic in content) and through this to reembrace the resistant capacity of critical culture.

It is a stark prospect and a difficult choice that not everyone in the design professions is equally free to make to the same degree, that is to say, the choice between going with the flow of the market or cultivating a self-conscious resistance along the lines of Ernst Bloch's projected hope, his evocation of the "not yet." Certainly living needs, as opposed to desires, demand to be met but surely not in such a way as to ruin the world for generations yet unborn.

1

Spectacle and Its Discontents; or, The Elusive Joys of Architainment

Luis Fernández-Galiano

The fall of the Berlin Wall closed one century and many debates. November 9, 1989, marked the end of the cold war and the end of the ideological rift that dominated almost the entire twentieth century. Democracy and the market, political and economic freedom won the day and the century—the century that in certain important ways began with the assassination in Sarajevo in 1914 that precipitated the First World War, and in equally key ways ended as thousands of East Germans peacefully walked into the West in a year that may become as historically significant as 1492 or 1789. And with the vanishing of that divided world, globalization takes command. Under the new regime, frontiers no longer divide rival empires: as in classical times, the new *limes,* or boundaries, of our *ecumene,* or habitable earth, mark the perimeter of the civilized world, one ruled by a single power that leaves only barbarians outside the gates. In the old order, two competing players conceived the planet as a chessboard whose squares had to be controlled, and the most remote corner could become strategic; once the game was over, large sections of the board were left out of the picture and have been slowly receding into the blurred distance of redundancy beyond the new city walls. Within the boundaries of our global society, tight and turbulent nets have developed, producing both interdependence and anxiety: a safety net that links ideas, institutions, and currencies, and a fishing net that dredges populations and certainties from the stillness of the ocean floor.

What kind of built environment can we expect within the boundaries of our global community? That of the dominant power, the United States, spread to the remaining territories of the ecumene, just as the Romans transferred their town planning, engineering, and architecture to the whole Mediterranean world. These new landscapes of wealth can be summarized in two words, *sprawl* and *spectacle*: a physical environment cluttered with construction and a symbolic universe devoured by the media. Under the sovereign rule of the consumer, the built environment is trivialized and thematized, but such is perhaps the price to pay for political and economic freedom, which carries in its wake urban and architectural freedom as an inevitable consequence. Many have mourned for the waning of highbrow architecture in a global context that fails to value excellence over popularity. In contrast, much of the best contemporary design does not ignore sprawl or spectacle but rather struggles to ride the wild wave of mass culture. And indeed, mass culture has become a synonym for global culture, because the tidal wave of mass taste has already engulfed the farthest shores of a world woven by the warp and woof of the instantaneous net that blurs identity, breeding uncertainty and rendering meaningless the comforting oxymoron of the *glocal*.

In the new panorama of McVillas and McBuildings, where architecture and entertainment are fused in museums and malls, downtowns and strips, theme parks and parking lots, what has vanished is *gravitas*. The *lightness* praised by Italo Calvino in *Six Memos for the Next Millennium*, his Charles Eliot Norton lectures written for but never delivered at Harvard, informs much architectural creation; heavy and tactile constructions are now considered archaic or elegiac. But if net portals fetch higher stock prices than established companies, why should the new buildings of the peripatetic and restless elite be more than wallpaper thin? When Yahoo is more valuable than Boeing, preaching in the desert for thickness and depth will only elicit guffaws. The new architecture may have its discontents, but this new architecture, this *architainment* of fleeting images and flashing screens, is out there, on offer in a NASDAQ of its own. The thin crust of its spread is disdained by some as a cancerous growth, viewed more equably by others as the immaterial membrane of a new species colonizing the earth. Metastasis or membrane, architainment seems to be here to stay, and the prophets of doom are regarded much as the princes of the market judge Federal Reserve Board Chairman Alan Greenspan: with outward reverence and inner disregard. If gravitas continues to figure in our concept of architecture, it does so largely as representation, which conveys more a nostalgia for materiality than an acknowledgment of the physical nature of buildings.

There are few recent works of such tactile presence as Herzog & de Meuron's Dominus Winery in Napa Valley or Peter Zumthor's Baths at Vals. To use Nietzsche's words, "stone is more stone than before" in the heavy basalt gabions of the winery, a work of exquisite detailing and refined rigor, one that filters light and air through its archaic lattice; and water is more water than before in the luminous cavern of the baths, where the thermal delight of the skin is echoed by the visual delight in the geometric labyrinth of layered gneiss stone. But a few weeks after being finished, both buildings had fallen prey to our voracity for images: the winery was featured on the cover of the *New York Times Magazine* as a backdrop for men's clothes, and the baths were used in the magazine *Wallpaper* as a setting for the display of fashion. Are the buildings fashion victims or trendsetters? The British magazine explains its name in a subtitle that belies a laconic program: "Wallpaper, the stuff that surrounds you." Gottfried Semper's *Bekleidung*—the building as clothing—has been turned into a wrapping for lifestyle, and those architectures most radically entrenched in materiality, tactility, and gravitas are most quickly pressed into the service of spectacle. How ironic, too, that this gravitas, accepted only as a sign, reappears as stubborn structural matter in works that most flaunt their light immaterial nature; I am thinking of the huge hidden trusses that keep in place the suspended volumes of MVRDV's Hannover Expo pavilion and or their WoZoCo apartments in Amsterdam, and of the tightly packed bundles of thick steel tubes that hold the floor plates and the blurred profile of Toyo Ito's Sendai Mediatheque.

Today, in fact, tactile matter and visual lightness are no more opposed than are the Apollonian boxes and Dionysian blobs that have served as polemical poles in recent debates about architectural form. Each has been incorporated into the process of the accelerated consumption of images that has reduced the shelf life of architecture from the season to the sigh. This symbolic obsolescence fuels a dazzling carousel with a dizzying variety of recombinant images, aimlessly drifting in an unpredictable flow, making appearances and exits in a haphazard kaleidoscope. French novelist Michel Houellebecq, in *The Elementary Particles* (2000), has used the metaphor of particles to refer to a world

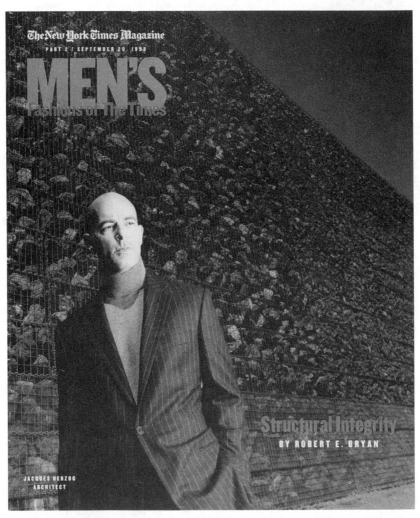

The New York Times Magazine, September 20, 1998: cover featuring architect Jacques Herzog in front of the completed Dominus Winery, Napa Valley, California. Photograph copyright Philip Dixon/New York Times.

of isolated individuals pursuing independent aims with mutual indifference, and he has poignantly described the deranged social landscape that results from this interpersonal isolation. We might perhaps extend his desolate view to the universe of artistic objects; we might even relate the proliferation of unconnected architectural images to the skeptical nihilism that underlies the Museum of Modern Art's centenary exhibitions and the arrangement of the twentieth-century collection in the new Tate Modern, wherein chronological and stylistic coherence have been eschewed in favor of presenting autonomous works in polite conversation. Architectural images may be scoring well in the game of fashion, a game whose only rule is that today's big thing is tomorrow's big yawn, but for a discipline that yearns for permanence, those goals can lead to nothing but an endgame.

Of course fashion rules the day, and profitable houses like Prada, Gucci, and Armani bankroll exhibitions at cash-hungry museums to benefit from the media coverage given to art conceived as entertainment, while architecture follows suit with the inevitable inertia of its longer time frames. Theme parks and art museums are increasingly joined by upscale retailers as patrons of high-profile architecture. In New York, the opening of the LVMH Tower (U.S. headquarters for the luxury goods purveyor Moët Hennessy Louis Vuitton) on 57th Street has allowed the company's CEO, Bernard Arnault, to share the glamour of architectural patronage already enjoyed by Disney's Michael Eisner or the Guggenheim's Thomas Krens. For LVMH, owner of trademarks like Christian Dior, Givenchy, Christian Lacroix, Guerlain, and Kenzo, the French architect Christian de Portzamparc has designed a conventional skyscraper, although one clad with a fractured reflective skin. This glamorous surface has been enough to unleash a torrent of praise from the local critical crowd, from Ada Louise Huxtable and Paul Goldberger to Herbert Muschamp and Joseph Giovannini. The French were the first to promote screen-printed glazing and immaterial facades (the latter famously exemplified by Jean Nouvel's Fondation Cartier) as *architecture médiatique*; still, one would expect New Yorkers to be a more resilient and skeptical lot when faced with Parisian chic. And soon New York will be the stage for the clash—or maybe the cross-pollination—of two influential strands of European architecture, the Dutch and the Swiss: the Office for Metropolitan Architecture and Herzog & de Meuron are jointly designing a hotel for Ian Schrager (the owner of several hotels designed by the Frenchman Philippe Starck, from the Royalton and Paramount in Manhattan to

St. Martins Lane in London, the latter a mix of boutique hotel and theme park). We are entitled to be curious about the outcome of this encounter between the surrealistic tendencies of Rotterdam and the material rigor of Basel in an American metropolis fascinated by European glamour.

And beyond the big city, the sprawl of spectacle is mirrored by the spectacle of sprawl, the land increasingly cluttered with the visual rubble of residential gluttony, with the bland and easy pastiches favored by the current nouveaux riches. "Postmodernism is almost all right" might as well be the slogan for the new landscapes of wealth being built all around the world. This architectural lingua franca was coined in the United States, a country that boasts five million millionaires (the *Economist* claims that if Great Britain was the first country to produce a mass middle class, the United States is the first to produce a mass upper class), but its banality reaches to the farthest edges of our prosperous ecumene of consumption. Wired by the nervous system of the Internet, this *Truman Show*–like world is a colossal narcissistic theater where only the stock market can create anxiety, and where only cyberviruses can cry wolf. The global environment is a paradoxical landscape of fiction and disorder, creating comedy within its boundaries and tragedy beyond them. After all, there is no great distance between a frontline art museum with a colossal Louise Bourgeois spider and a blue-chip theme park with Mouseketeers and Space Mountains, or at least no greater distance than that between the new global shopping and entertainment centers and the abandoned fringes and desolated peripheries of the market.

This may well sound like an elegy for lost gravitas in architecture and a vanished *romanitas* in society—an effort to exorcise contemporary demons, and as such about as useful as garlic to repel vampires, and maybe even akin to that tradition of critical complaint that inspired Paul Valéry to write of intellectuals: "Cette espèce pourtant se plaint; donc elle existe" (However, this type complains, and therefore exists). There are indeed specters that haunt architecture, but in a society in which real crime forms the content of TV shows, and in which the poor buy lottery tickets that finance the opera houses of the wealthy, there is not much harm in disregarding the teleprompters, overlooking the received ideas, and being somehow indifferent to public taste. Indifference is not disdain; after all, even flat-earth lunatics can find comfort in the fact that the universe has been found to be more or less . . . flat. "We must be open-minded, but not so open-minded that our brains drop out," goes the joke. The intellectual venture capital of many an architect has been invested in the new casino economy of fashion; let those discontented with architainment opt for safer shares and safer shores.

2000

2

Less for Less Yet: On Architecture's Value(s) in the Marketplace

Michael Benedikt

Why ask about architecture's values or the value of architecture? Are we in any doubt about either? Certainly, architectural monthlies and the major newspapers find no shortage of sharp new buildings to show. Recondite history and theory books continue to be published, enough to satisfy a generation of junior faculty (and then some), and all serve to substantiate our positive opinion of architecture's heritage and importance. Lectures and exhibitions and professional meetings abound. We give and get design awards. And for the more retiring among us there is always *Architectural Digest* (covertly examined), travel to the villas and gardens of Europe, and new books with reassuring titles like *The Architectural Photograph*.

Indeed, it is possible for architects to live entirely inside this World of Architecture, which is a state of mind, without ever leaving it. It is possible for architects to drive through the overturned garbage can that is a large part of the American built environment, tsk-tsking about the averageness of other architects and the rapacity of developers, without ever thinking that the condition of the modern world is due at least *partially* to what the "best" and most prominent architects have done, have allowed, and have come earnestly to believe over the past fifty years. This is why we should ask about architectural values.

And what do we, or they—the "best" architects—believe? I shall keep the list short and deliberately conventional: that architecture is for people; that integrity and honesty of expression are a virtue; that form follows function; that simplicity is beautiful; that cheap doesn't necessarily mean bad or ugly; that creativity is the architect's chief gift to society; that indoors and outdoors should be melded; that shaping or manipulating space is the essence of what architects do; that the grid is rational; that the world is "speeding up" and architecture should/must follow (corollary: that advances in technology offer possibilities for architecture that should not be passed up); that together with our consultants we understand completely what a building is and does. Every one of these essentially Modernist beliefs, held as a value, is problematic for architecture's value. Every one of them (except, perhaps, the first) has caused more harm than good to the environment and to our profession.

Consider the idea that creativity is our chief gift to society.[1] The first thing to challenge, even if one accepts the proposition, is whether architects are indeed all that creative. Look around and decide. Consider too that several other fields can claim as much creativity as we do, from artists on the one hand to politicians on the other. But these are easy shots. More subtle and far-reaching is the dilemma that basing our personal and professional reputations on creativity greatly weakens our negotiating power when all the parties that have a say in the design of the environment are sitting around the same table. Imagine, for instance, that an impasse has arisen. Here is the engineer; here is the owner; here are the contractor, the city official, the neighborhood group representative, the financier, and the architect. Someone has to give. Who will have to be "flexible"? Who will have to go back to the drawing board because she is "so creative"? You guessed it.

Consider another situation: a client comes to an architect with a tight budget and an ambitious project. The architect believes (as he was taught at school) that cheap does not necessarily mean bad or ugly, that creativity is his gift to society, and that if he does not take the job, some lesser architect will. Rare is the architect—and then only in the best of economic times—who will politely show the client the door, informing him that a Mercedes for the price of a Volkswagen *cannot be had*. Most architects would rather give it a go; do *something*! Is he not creative? Cannot cheap things be beautiful? Is this not a democracy where even the modestly well off can get to have (my) Good Design? And later, when the project has fallen apart logistically, or pieces are lopped off, or finishes are downgraded, or fees are not paid because the budget is being overshot, who does the architect *really* blame, despite what he tells others? Himself, of course. He was not "creative" enough.

Creativity is probably the single worst idea with which architects could associate themselves. And yet "the chance to be creative" is today the foremost reason students give for wanting to become architects. No teacher will discourage this goal or disabuse them of this value—or at least replace it with other values, such as the achievement of excellence or knowledge or dignity or power—not just because "being creative" has become tantamount in our time to a human right, but because the ideal of material design creativity, of redemption through the combination of art and engineering, goes back to the very raison d'être of Modern architecture and its promise to humanity. Choose against creativity and we are condemned to make buildings unequal to the challenges of the Modern World. Or so we children of the Bauhaus were told.

I am writing this essay in a three-hundred-year-old building; the light is wonderful, and the electricity courses through my computer just fine, and the phone is at hand, and the toilet flushes like a dream. The argument that to build "the old way" was to build inadequately for the Challenges of the Modern World was just so much rhetoric, serving best those who stood to profit from increasing urban land values and decreasing per-square-foot construction costs, from wringing out more rent, building highways, and receiving architectural commissions from newly monied industrialists.

In Germany, as everywhere in western Europe in the late nineteenth century, the countryside was emptying into the cities as the basis for economic development changed from agriculture to industry. Workers needed to be (ware)housed, factories built and manned. The physical destruction caused by the First World War, along with the financial crises that followed,[2] allowed the prewar aims of the Werkbund—that is, rationalized construction as conceived under the banner of Modernity—to take hold and take over. By 1945, at the end of the Second World War, Modernism, the architecture of crisis and of recovery, had become the only game in town, a second-growth species that would not go away. In America, undamaged by war and now home to Walter Gropius and Ludwig Mies van der Rohe, civilian construction accounted for 11 percent of the gross national product in 1950. By 1990 its share had dropped to 7.9 percent. The rate of building production over the same period increased from 600 million to 3,500 million square feet per annum. Thus, a 600 percent increase in construction volume was achieved with a 25 percent decrease in GNP expenditure. Efficiency? Enviable "returns to scale"? This is the viewpoint of the economist and also of those who do not see that the product itself has changed. Clearly, we are progressively directing relatively less of our total wealth and effort to infrastructural and architectural quality. This reflects our national values directly. Over the same period, the share of GNP represented by the banking, real estate, entertainment, and communication sectors of the economy grew in precisely the opposite direction. The conclusion? Our environment has become ever more commodified, ever more the subject of short-term investment, income generation, and resale rather than of lifelong dwelling or long-term city making.[3]

But we cannot blame "the market." Most of the "nice old buildings" that ordinary people like and that we say we can no longer afford to build—with their high ceilings, operable windows, well-defined rooms, solid walls, pleasing decoration, and dignified demeanor—were built in a market context and were not cheap. Indeed, they were more expensive for their owners to build and finance in their own day than they would be to build and finance again in ours. What *has* changed is the national will to direct attention, labor, and resources to architecture specifically and the built environment generally, be it through markets or governments. And one reason for this change has been the relinquishment by architects of their role—indeed duty—in upholding standards and modes of discourses about design that ordinary people can understand and that produce buildings that people *want* to live and work in for reasons other than the fact that they are new.

In societies at peace that can maintain free markets, people can get what they want; what they want depends on how successfully their needs and values are addressed by competing producers. With a modicum of prosperity, people have choices. This is the context in which architecture, as an industry, broadly conceived, has become less and less able to deliver a superior, evolving, and popularly engaging product that can compete with other, more successful products—with cars, music, movies, sports, and travel, to name a few. And the less successfully architecture has competed with these diverse "growth industries," the less architects have been entrusted with time and money to perform work on a scale and with a quality that could, perhaps, turn things around.

I say "perhaps," because it is far from certain that the knowledge architects currently have and the values architects currently subscribe to could build a world people really wanted, given *any* amount of time and money. Many people are afraid of hiring architects, especially those well known by other architects. Now *that* is a sobering thought, and if there were no exceptions to it, we would all have to pack it in. But let us not use these exceptions as a screen between ourselves and the world—that is, between what we sometimes do well and what remains to be done, which becomes evident if we will only look out the window.

It is ironic, yet somehow predictable, that Modernism—fruit of the economic ruin of Europe by two world wars, enemy of aristocratic privilege, champion of efficiency over sentiment—should finally, with the Neo-Modernism of today, become the prestige style of the rich even as much of America struggles to ignore its consequences: windowless suburban high schools hardly more comfortable than minimum-security prisons; a despoiled landscape of shopping malls, billboards, and deserted reminders of obsolete manufacturing prowess; wire-crossed skies; housing "projects"; weedy lots called parks; and for relief, gigantic blocks of mirrored clouds floating on lawns hiding acres of Wonder-thin office space, fed by interstates thundering through canyons, around hills, and over and past tinderbox cottages nuzzled by broken cars or too-perfect *Truman Show*–esque enclaves of refugees and retirees.

No wonder people go to the movies, where they can see what happens when someone takes days to get the light right.

Take another value-cum-credo. *Form follows function.* Functionalism was a poison pill, swallowed first by well-meaning architectural writers drawing (mistakenly) on the "design" intentions of nature (which is, in fact, profligately rococo), second by ambitious architects with an eye to getting more work from businessmen using social Darwinism ("survival of the fittest") as an operating principle, and third by ordinary persons, who hardly needed convincing that Progress depended on the power of machines to be ruthlessly focused in purpose.[4] Instead of inspiring investigation into what buildings do, which is as delicate and multifarious and easy to misunderstand as nature's real complexity, functionalism helped eliminate all aspects of architecture for which a robust health-and-safety or cost-saving rationale could not be mustered and forced across the desk of an impassive banker.

I am certainly not the first to decry functionalism. The Postmodern

movement in architecture—1965–85, R.I.P.—exhausted itself in re-
buking the form-follows-function dictum, or at least in desperate reinterpretation of it. But it was too late. The ceiling of expectations as
to what architecture could and should and would achieve was already
lowered, ratcheted down by decades of efficiency-talk and rationality-
talk on the consumer end, and, on the production end, by the failure
to develop fresh technology that could lower construction costs fast
enough to free up money for a round of ambitious and complex design. Those small economies that could be technologically effected
(lightweight structural and wall systems, for example) were quickly
hijacked by rentiers and financiers, and by clients with better things
to do with their money. Thus, the economic ceiling lowered another
notch. Every architect who, through estimable creativity and self-
application, found a cheaper way to build, became an example, will-
ing or not, of what the next architect should be able to "achieve" too.
With project budgeting thus cast as an exercise in starving the building
(if not the architect), it was no wonder that all that earnest architectural effort—all the travel to Europe to sketch Rome in the 1970s, all
the poring over Palladio and breast-beating about Gropius and Mies
(who misled us!), the reading of Venturi and Blake and looking for
complexity and contradiction in old plans and then simulating it in
ours—should have resulted largely in commercial co-option, pastiche,
academicism, and another round of despair about architecture's uses.

What has been our latest answer? So far, three (major) movements in
little more than a decade, overlapping of course. First Deconstruction,
then computerization, and now the return to Modernism in one of two
forms: the elite, art-world form of Minimalism, or the brash, fuck-you
form of Undecorated Garage with Large Glass. None of these movements is likely to enable architects to transform the cynical mess that
is the postwar environment into a place where everyone is pleased to be
a native envied by a tourist, including, when he is at home, the tourist.

Consider Deconstruction. As practiced by Zaha Hadid, Peter Eisen-
man, Daniel Libeskind, or Frank Gehry, it will continue to get press.
But what these architects do does not follow Kant's "categorical imperative": to work according to principles that others can work according to as well. Their architecture is premised on crashingly obvious exceptionalism, and this cannot be a way of making cities. The
complex and delicate experience of *joy-in-inhabitation,* to which we
all have a right, comes from a thousand subtleties of position and color
and view and touch located in the DNA, so to speak, of traditional

city making. This kind of complexity—the visual and spatial equivalent of a composition by Chopin, say—was still known, at some level, by the notable pre-Modern architects of both Europe and America but was largely extinct by 1945. Where to plant a tree, how to make a terrace, how to shape and open a window . . . these manifest a complexity that can only be evolved; it cannot be simulated, represented, transformed, or produced ab initio by formal games and explorations, no matter how elaborate, literate, or "logical." Schönberg cannot be a model for architects. Nor can Derrida as he is currently read.

Computerization is not a style, of course, but it is a new way of conceiving buildings, and almost imperceptibly it leads architects to make value judgments they might not otherwise make. This happens even as—indeed precisely *because*—architects protest that CAD is "just a new drafting tool" enabling them to "offer better service." To their credit, the architects mentioned above use the computer to permit greater complexity of form and depth of design exploration as well as to attempt greater precision and ambition in construction.[5] But the computer is not being used so skillfully by the majority of architects responsible for what you see on the drive to the mall. The computer is being used as conventionally used in business: to increase productivity, that is, to stimulate more output per unit of labor input. A building that ten years ago would have taken ten draftsmen one year to draw, might now take three draftsmen eight months to draw. Once digitized, details from old projects can be seamlessly incorporated into new projects.[6] Documents can easily be updated as construction progresses and further economies are found. And so on.

The efficiencies that computers afford raise a critical question: who is benefiting from the increased productivity and the time saved? I would venture that it is not the architect. I would venture that intense market competition between architects, focused on service-for-fee and the ability to control costs, has passed these productivity-won savings cleanly along to clients, and that architects have not, with these savings, bought one minute more of their own time to spend on the design or refinement of their buildings. Indeed, so seductive is the computer's capacity to copy files hither and thither and to render "space(s)" in no time at all, that I would venture that *less* time is being spent in design, profession-wide, than ever before. Moreover, the design being done is done more and more on the computer—I have yet to meet a practicing architect under fifty who is not proud of this recent accomplishment— despite the plain-as-day fact that the compositional tools provided by

CAD software cannot match the fluidity and serendipity and delicacy of hand-guided pencil on molecularly noisy paper, let alone the capacity of this "old" medium for recording the accumulation of thought over time. Add to this CAD's inherent reluctance to represent land forms fluidly—the curves and cuts and twisted surfaces, the plants, the wildness and color.

And so the economizing continues, round after round, the average architect delivering less and so being asked to deliver less for less yet: three-dimensional shadows of real buildings.

And Modernism? Modern architecture rode to the rescue in Germany and France after the First World War, remobilizing idled factories from the production of munitions to the production of lightbulbs and sinks and awning windows for the sanitary housing of the struggling lower classes. Modernism delivered again at midcentury, transmogrified into the International Style. By then it had become the architectural recipe for sending clearinghouses of money and trade mushrooming skyward in every nation, for housing thousands of people at once in great gulps of construction (the concrete frame, the glass and steel, the "plaza"). And this occurred not just in New York and Stuttgart, but also in Montevideo, Johannesburg, Athens, Tel Aviv, Hong Kong, Moscow, Mexico City . . . cities all over the world whose postwar architectural character to this day amounts to poured-in-place graph paper with occasional awnings, roaring with the sound of exhaust pipes.

Can Modernism now rescue us from having earlier been rescued by Modernism? Does it have within its genes—within its doctrines and methods and pleasures—permutations as yet unexplored? Perhaps. But two developments (at least) are required for such discoveries to make a perceptible difference to the environment of more than a handful of connoisseurs. First, another quantum leap "forward" in the technology of construction, in terms of cost and speed. Such a development accounted for the widespread adoption of Modernism in the first place, initially in promise (1900–27), then in reality (1930–present).[7] Modernist buildings are simply more "cost efficient," especially when land is expensive. But small and steady cost reductions will not do. The savings that these generate (and there are many if you look carefully) are abducted by developers as fast as they can be devised. Only the faster-than-expected adoption of a radically cheaper way to design and build will allow architects to capture and invest the savings in better design and new stylistic maneuvers. The risk is that if these maneuvers do not soon produce a kind of building that appeals strongly to the public on other than economic grounds, then competitive market "forces"—reflecting nothing more sinister, really, than people's decision to (continue to) spend their money elsewhere—will siphon off everything "unnecessary." Construction budget setters will prevail once more, leaving architects in the long run worse off than before, with even fewer means with which to pursue their art.

The second required development is another round of propaganda to convince the public once again that (even) Less is More:[8] less materiality, froufrou, and landscaping; thinner doors and walls and veneers; fewer surfaces that need waxing, polishing, or painting; less cloth and textile, less print and pattern, fewer things that fold or move; less trim; tighter lots; less contact with ground, air, and climate. As with diets and weight loss and health foods, people must be convinced of the merits of further leanness and purity, that the white-on-white emptiness of the art museum *sans the art* represents an ideal place in which to live and work, that the bride stripped bare is more comely than the bride. (Offering them folds and shards of nothingness, or great white whalelike spaces, will only rub in the vacuity of the whole exercise.)

Of course, the trouble here is that in architecture as in fashion, minimalism yields pleasure in proportion to its expense, requiring great precision in construction, high levels of finish quality, and carefully controlled lighting (not to say a certain attitude from the user) in order to be valuable. But it is not likely that this value will be achieved; it is more likely that the present embrace of luxo-minimalism by elites will culturally legitimate minimalism of a more virulent, ersatz sort. For soon (if not already) building developers and furniture designers and fixture makers will have the "permission" of a Pawson or Gucci to consign even more of the desirable complexities, comforts, solidities, and physical amenities of buildings to the category of "bell" or "whistle."

Architecture as a T-shirt for living in? Will this sell? Maybe, but for all the wrong reasons, and certainly with sorry results.

Earlier I said that in market societies, people get what they want. This is not quite right. They get what they want *most*. People who shop at Wal-Mart do not want to kill off their old downtown; they want to save a few dollars, have a wider choice of goods, and so forth. Who can blame them? People want cheap energy and low taxes. Who doesn't? But in pursuit of what we want we get dead rivers, cracked sidewalks, dumb kids, and crime. Individually rational market decisions can have collective outcomes that few, including those who

John Pawson Architects, Pawson House, Notting Hill, London, England, 1994. Photograph copyright Richard Glover/VIEW. "Minimalism yields pleasure in proportion to its expense."

make such decisions, are happy about. (Let the *other* person send the kids to a school that needs help, let *them* shop at the corner store, let *them* stay off the road at peak traffic times. . . .) Social scientists are at a loss to recommend how to resolve these difficulties without limiting people's freedom or democratic rights.[9]

When it comes to architecture, we are confronted with this dynamic writ large. Move among ordinary people and you will find that still, after decades of publicity and Pritzker Prizes ("the what prize?"), almost nobody likes "modern architecture." Sure, people are grateful for air conditioning and good plumbing, but they have disliked everything else about modern buildings and the modern city for sixty years! And yet they are paying for them, living in them, working in them by the millions, dispirited to be doing so, and, when not merely resigned, they are blaming everyone but themselves: developers, politicians, builders, city officials, and, not the least, architects.

But as with Wal-Mart, the truth is more complicated. With every dollar and every vote, and with myriad individual market and political decisions, ordinary people have passed up the goods that architecture has been able to offer. Passed them up with an occasional sigh, of course, but passed them up nonetheless for the more compelling seductions of movies and TV, on the one hand, and for more urgent needs, like health and freedom and jobs, on the other. No one *wants* to see nice buildings and parks and streets disappear, but each of us wants the *other* guy (or his taxes or profits) to build something nice for us all.

It is said that market forces are impersonal, but the upshot is that, in the marketplace at least, architects have been outflanked and out-maneuvered by the purveyors of stronger medicines with better stories. Architects have not fought back effectively but instead continue to sacrifice themselves on an altar of their own making in loyalty (or is it submission?) to the religion that still, albeit with increasing difficulty and infighting, organizes their schools. I refer, of course, to Modernism, Post and Neo.

To find answers to the question of architecture's value, answers adequate to any hoped-for revaluation of the architectural enterprise in the next century, we will need to go beyond the essentially art-historical scholarship that has been our steady diet for so many years now and take up a whole new kind of theorizing and explaining.

Such new theory should explore the circle route from architecture through cosmology, thermodynamics, and complex systems, through biology and evolutionary theory, through social psychology and psychology, through economics and economic history and back again to architecture, to show that the activities of designing and making buildings and of organizing and forming and planting the land are so deeply rooted in the doings of the universe that they must elaborate themselves alongside all other human activities, not self-simplify and flatten, if we are to be happy on this planet. Life, whose increase is called *value*, peeks out of a thousand masks, each of which grows in complexity and in organization. One of them is architecture.

New theory must trace the lines of money and information and influence that coalesce to form first a single building and then buildings of different kinds (equivalent to the birth of new organisms, call it architectural embryology). Further, the case must be made that a national dedication to environmental health, urban vitality, and fine architecture will contribute to the continued economic growth and development of this country and others in the twenty-first century. What better use is there for our prosperity? What better organizer of social purposes and generator of further wealth? What better legacy for our children?

New theory must crisscross the parched fields of environment-and-behavior and environmental design research, thirty years' worth gone unnoticed by architects, in search of new approaches that will stand up to use. It must find powerful new or forgotten ways of talking about the intimate connections between people and places, perhaps by rereading Bachelard and Borges, Freud and Proust—familiar territory, to be sure but trodden firm.

What *needs* does architecture serve? I wager that the reader cannot make a list both useful and satisfying.

New theory must model the larger implications of architecture's digitization beyond the potential for creating extraordinary form.[10] For soon those who commission architecture, and even those who "consume" it, will wake up fully to the reality that most buildings, within a type, have no inherent reason to differ from other buildings, from place to place. The architect's already tenuous status as a custom tailor, based on the flattery of supposing that every building is properly a "unique response" to a unique site and program, will surely be challenged if not ridiculed once computers guide machinery directly from "drawings," which can themselves be parameterized and, if necessary, modularized and commoditized and traded to make buildings that will never be seen next to each other. Recombinant architecture? Why not? Think of what digital sampling has done to (for?) the production of music.

New theory must make detailed surveys of what architecture has discarded in the wholesale handing over of everything remotely scientific and quantitative to consulting engineers. Acoustics, light, lighting, air quality and air movement, heating, cooling . . . what engineers know and do about these things (I exempt structural engineers from this critique) has become so narrow and formulaic that their expertises together can be said to form a chain of islands separated from each other, and from the mainland of design, by oceans of ignorance about architectural phenomena. These phenomena were once the chief source of architecture's value and were attended to "automatically," with, as it were, the DNA of traditional models. Today few architects know about such things. Evaluating the glare from a window, assessing the resilience of a floor, modeling the coherence of interior air flow or the balance of radiant to ambient heat, simulating the pattern of sound reflections down the halls and in the rooms of an ordinary building (not a concert hall or auditorium), analyzing patterns of privacy and exposure, and understanding how these factors work together to create good quality in a place, value in architecture: these are activities that do not currently form the stuff of architectural practice (let alone produce design fame), and they are taught hurriedly (if at all) by the least design-adept teachers at school. This is not a call for empiricism per se. This is not about "creating a body of architectural knowledge." This is about raising a submerged Atlantis of architectural sensibility, a realm of facts and insights that can support popular connoisseurship of the qualities of buildings equal to that devoted to the valuation of music, cars, and movies. To take this material seriously, technically *and* poetically, will help us to make a powerful case that architecture matters at all and can produce genuine effects that people will notice, appreciate, measure, value, and ultimately demand.

So begins but does not end a list of projects to accomplish architecture's revaluation. If you have been persuaded that work on them must start, then the mission of this essay has been achieved.

1999

Notes

1. A variant on this belief, 1970s vintage: architects are "problem solvers."
2. Germany's predicament was exacerbated by American foreign policy. Presidents Wilson, Coolidge, and Hoover insisted that war debt owed to the United States by the allied victors be paid regardless of whether these countries—chiefly England, France, Belgium, Italy—received or forgave Germany its debt to them in war reparations. With no choice but to insist on repayments, the allies ensured that Germany would remain economically crippled and spiritually humiliated for more than a decade, which germinated extremist social ideologies of all kinds.
3. Patricia Mainardi in *The End of the Salon* (New York: Cambridge University Press, 1993) provides an excellent analysis of the importance of economic and market considerations in accounting for the origins of Modernism in art—art, for better or worse, as commodity.
4. The phrase "form follows function" has an interesting provenance. Begun as an Enlightenment idea espoused by eighteenth-century Italian philosophers Lodoli and Milizia and informing Boullée and Ledoux in the nineteenth century, the phrase enters the mind of Italophile American Horace Greenough, whence it circulates in the Chicago School of the 1890s with Louis Sullivan and young Frank Lloyd Wright, and forms the watchword of the Chicago Exposition of 1893, which is visited by Adolf Loos (who also meets with Sullivan), whence it returns to Europe with Loos and combines (in the mind of young Le Corbusier, for one, who meets with Loos on the latter's return)

with the teachings of English socialist William Morris as filtered and transformed by critics Herman Muthesius and Karl Scheffler, who were influential in the prewar Werkbund in Germany (actually founded by Muthesius) and who followed closely the career and thought of Peter Behrens, architect to the industrialist AEG. It then establishes itself as the unquestioned truth and unquestionable motivation, dominating all others, of European Modernism, and then, with the help of Wright, two world wars, and an army of bow-tied polemicists, of modernism, small *m* or large, everywhere since. It is a tragedy of some proportion that "form follows function" is true neither of nature nor of economic development.

5. I believe that they are after the *wrong* sort of complexity, but that is another matter.

6. Indeed, I predict a market in digital construction details, perhaps whole building pieces like auditoria or staircases, traded between firms, or perhaps marketed by McGraw-Hill.

7. These dates are very rough, of course. I consider the Weissenhofseidlung in Stuttgart in 1927 to be the watershed event. Others might consider the International Werkbund Exhibition in Berlin in 1931.

8. I do not necessarily mean less interior *space* per person or household, at least not in North America, where new tract houses anyway are getting larger and plainer (with better appliances).

9. See, for example, Mancur Olson, *The Logic of Collective Action* (Cambridge: Harvard University Press, 1971) or Thomas Schelling, *Micromotives and Macrobehavior* (New York: Norton, 1978); and see Douglas Heckathorn, "The Dynamics and Dilemmas of Collective Action," *American Sociological Review* 61, no. 2 (April 1996): 250–78, for a recent, I think breakthrough, analysis of how Prisoner's Dilemmas, Tragedy of the Commons, and other strategic patterns of behavior challenge any strong belief in the fairness, or even desirability, of the outcomes of the market order.

10. Which is *not* to say that extraordinary form will not turn out to be an important contributor to architecture's revaluation. Here I look to the recent work of Frank Gehry, of course, but also to Marcos Novak of UCLA and Kas Oosterhuis from the Netherlands, Neil Denari at SCI-Arc, and others.

3

Brand Aid;
or, The Lexus and the
Guggenheim (Further Tales
of the Notorious B.I.G.ness)
Michael Sorkin

It is only natural that the Guggenheim should be at the Venetian. Fabled Peggy, after all, dwelled by the Grand Canal. The easy comparison, though, is less than apposite: this Guggenheim is not to that one as the Venetian is to Venice.

The Vegas Guggenheim is, in fact, two, both designed by Rem Koolhaas. A small Cor-Ten box with several dozen very good pictures from the Guggenheim and the Hermitage opens off the main entrance to the hotel with all modesty. Out behind the casino is a much larger space of semi-industrial character in which the Frank O. Gehry & Associates–designed, BMW-sponsored "Art of the Motorcycle" exhibition now sits. Both components of the museum house their respective shows gracefully. The rust-patinaed steel walls by the lobby are repatinaed with wax and match nicely the polychrome stone floors of the hotel. The big room makes no particular pretension to being more than that. Neither gallery reads as an object—hopeless trying to compete with the pirate ship across the street.

Were photography not tenaciously forbidden, I would have tried for a shot out of one of the two narrow windows in the steel box. Past the Picasso, through the glass and protective grating, the mock Campanile and Ducal Palace of the Venetian rise to meet. At the end of the long perspective, the top of another hotel is visible, its electric sign reading

"Mirage." The view, of course, is totally Vegas. The simulacra. The tackiness. The pretension. The brands.

Branding is the quintessence of the new Vegas, and profligate signifiers dance to the tune. It is not so much that the idea of the brand is extended but that the concatenation is so extreme. Indeed, Vegas is the museum of branding, with its row of hotels named after Paris, New York, Luxor, Venice, Mandalay, Bellagio—hypertrophied but familiar evocations of place—recalling antebellum mansions or yachts named for some fondly remembered honeymoon spot, stuffed with artificial charm.

The motorcycles fit the paradigm well. Every example in the "Art of the Motorcycle" is a brand-name factory product, no room given, for example, to customization—to the popular transformation of the object. Indeed, the only bike that comes close is a reproduction (the one nonarchival item in the show) of the red, white, and blue customized Harley from *Easy Rider* (the original having been stolen years ago). I followed a group of aging bikers—dressed to the nines in flamboyant self-assembled gear—through the gallery, witness to the *real* art of the motorcycle. My thought was that their interaction with brand

Rem Koolhaas, entrance to Guggenheim Hermitage Museum, Las Vegas, Nevada, October 2001. Photograph by David Heald; copyright Guggenheim Museum.

Rem Koolhaas, Guggenheim Hermitage Museum, The Art of the Motorcycle exhibit, Las Vegas, Nevada, 2001. Photograph by David Heald; copyright Guggenheim Museum.

was loving but resistant. But it was tough not to be put in mind of the bloody fight between rival gangs the previous week in nearby Laughlin, where three bikers wound up dead.

In a catalog essay of blithe pomposity, Thomas Krens—director of the Guggenheim, famed for riding his chopper to the office—cites and then discards Walter Benjamin's distinction between the auratic original and the mechanically reproduced copy as "irrelevant in today's discourse." He is, of course, simply congratulating himself for the boldness of the idea of exhibiting motorcycles in an art museum, as if that were a remotely original idea. This dissembling, however, is also a distraction from his real innovation: soliciting corporations—like BMW, Giorgio Armani, or Hugo Boss—to sponsor "shows" of their own products, turning museums into boutiques and—with perfect business logic—the boutiques into franchises.

The match of Rem and Krens—two tall men with flat affects—is a great one: both are selling the same product: products. "Shopping is arguably the last remaining form of public activity," opines Koolhaas.[1] And so we shop for Picassos and Kandinskys, for Harleys and Yamahas, for Prada shoes and Bulgari brooches, all under the aura of the covetable pots of gold at the end of the fleeting rainbows glistening about the roulette tables and the high-stakes slots. Just as the way out of the museum leads through the shop, the exit from the casino is lined with boutiques and museums. At the motorcycle exhibition, the stairway is painted in Prada's signature chartreuse to reinforce the point. The retina is the point of sale: to see is to buy. In contemporary "casino capitalism," citizenship is a credit line, democracy a crapshoot.

The Guggenheim has a track record here. Joseba Zulaika quotes a city councilman in Bilbao worrying—in the wake of the decision to invest $500 per capita on the museum—that the decision was like "gambling in a casino."[2] That horse came in. The merger of art, shopping, and gambling also has a track record. Here, the innovator is Steve Wynn, whose Bellagio hotel (now sold to Kirk Kerkorian) was the standard-setter for the merger of high-end shopping ("the best assortment on the planet"), "gaming" (the new owners have reportedly removed the receptacles that had formerly muted to an elegant hush the sound of money tumbling from the Bellagio's slots), and, of course, the art collection (now decamped to Wynn's new Desert Inn).

To create the success of any commercial multiple, the brand is critical. Given his own reluctance to engage any nonquantitative criteria of quality and his conflation of consumption and nature, Koolhaas holds the concept in high esteem, elevating it to the core of his architectural ideology, something capable of subsuming all other values, including the political. And he can get huffy about it. As he remarked in a recent interview in the *New York Times* about his European Union–sponsored design for a new EU flag,

> Basically I think the discussion about what brands are is held on an incredibly primitive level. Particularly the American perception of what brand is, namely something that is reduced to its essence and can never be changed. I think that is a very limited form of branding. What we have been trying to do with Prada, for instance, is instead of trying to reduce it to its essence, we try to stretch it, so that more becomes possible instead of less. And that's exactly the same idea that we're trying to introduce for Europe. It extends the repertoire of possibilities instead of shrinking it.[3]

But what is the subtle, nuanced, nonessentialist version of branding alluded to here? Thomas Frank, in his *One Market under God,* describes the allure of the new market order and the rise of its avatars, Rem's progenitors:

> Just as the democratized, soulful corporation had arisen to resolve the problems of the hierarchical, elitist corporation, so a new breed of marketing thinker proposed a new conception of the brand. To think of the brand as a static thing, as a rock of Gibraltar or one of the great books, was to miss its dynamic nature. The brand, according to the new cognoscenti, was a relationship, a thing of nuance and complexity, of irony and evasion. It was not some top-down affair, some message to be banged into consumers' heads. The brand was a conversation, an ongoing dialogue between companies and the people. The brand was a democratic thing, an edifice that the people had helped build themselves simply by participating in the market. The brand, in short, was us.[4]

Frank describes with acerbic precision the emergence of a new "discipline" within the field of advertising—"Account Planning"—that promised "to restore legitimacy to the brand."[5] The frightening reach and vagueness of the concept are summed up in a British pamphlet introducing account planning to the uninitiated: "Advertising is a means of contributing meaning and values that are necessary and useful to people in structuring their lives, their casual relationships, and their rituals."[6] The imperative for rebranding advertising as account planning sprang from a climate in which the average American—exposed to a million advertising messages a year—was becoming skeptical about commercial claims and deafened by the din. The conclusion: only a re-conceptualization of the brand would allow products to "break out." This demanded a fresh intellectual apparatus. Frank notes the infusion of anthropological concepts into account planning, not to mention the large number of fashionably dressed lapsed graduate students who were bringing the lessons of Lévi-Strauss to Levi Strauss. The anthropological style of studied disengagement (Michael Hardt and Antonio Negri call anthropology "the most important academic discipline in the production of alterity"), with its sense of superiority to its subject, is pure Koolhaas.[7]

This inflated concept of brand informs the approaches of both Rem and the Guggenheim, and both have been highly successful in making their marks in a crowded—or expanded—field.[8] In a recent TV commercial the camera pans around a silver Lexus parked in front of the titanium Guggenheim. "I like to look at things of beauty," says the Renzo Piano look-alike actor poised between sedan and museum. The Lexus is a fine car. Bilbao is a fine building. The conversation is genuine. The products are well placed, mutually reinforcing.

It does seem, though, that more than one thing is going on here. Certainly the idea of associating the product with something held in high regard—like Catherine Deneuve or Bilbao—is Advertising 101. How else to sell soap? For architecture, though, the strategy of association also represents a handy back door for the resuscitation of style as a category of judgment. While this is good news for sheepish stylists, it is non-neutral, placing expression in the service of particular values. The grafting of the anthropological model reinforces the idea of the neutrality of the brand as well as its proliferation ("These people are different, therefore let us sell our products differently. Indeed, let us identify even more differences to sell.") But the business model—the real agenda—for the Guggenheim (or any other branding operation) is scarcely disinterested. It entails the sale of both advertising and product and seeks to establish the superiority—or at least the utility—of what's on offer. This provides the opportunity for the introduction of another standard of judgment, the curatorial, affirming the role of the tastemaker as the ultimate agent of brand. Style, as Stephen Brown notes, is the *substance* of postmodernity and thus must be accounted for by the authorities.[9] And, of course, celebrity is the main measure of authority in Brandworld.

Such standards remain usefully slippery. Even today—thirty years into postmodernity—functionalism is still the analytical default for determining architectural value. The form-follows-function formula is no less aesthetic for locating the value of visuality in the criterion of use. Of course, for architecture the relationship has generally been fraudulent, just an excuse for a shriveled system of taste. The legacy remains, however. Just as Koolhaas promotes his own brand with a blizzard of statistics, photos of the "real" world, and a weary sense of globalism's inescapable surfeit and waste as the only legitimate field of architectural action, the New Urbanists—with their own megalomaniac formulas of uniformity—create their slightly "different" Vegas of "traditional" architecture based on its association with the imagined reality of bygone happinesses. Their tunes may differ, but both are lyricists for the ideological master narrative that validates and celebrates the imperial machine. Like architecture, politics plays in the realm of symbols. The architecture of Vegas—in which the creative likes of Koolhaas or Gehry are trivial players—does reflect a larger reformulation of the profession's model of practice. European Modernism based its fantasy of self on the idea of production. Although architects may not have had genuinely strong affinities with the working class, they did promote an identification of architecture with the industrialization that produced it. Whether this was simply in the mechanical appearance of buildings, the idea of mass housing, or even the idea of factory production, the aim was to wrest architecture from the ethereal and unquantifiable realms of art and place it on a terrain where argument and quality would cleave to rational, objective standards.

Behind this lay a set of values—including such quaint notions as equality and justice—that were adduced as the ultimate rationale for subsuming architecture under the category of mass production. Modernism's focus on working-class housing implied a politics of distribution, a largely unspoken socialism of universal access to basic necessities. But the mode of production under which most modernists flourished was anything but egalitarian. Indeed, the rapid conversion of this fragile ideology into no more than style (an oft-told tale) was the signal of this basic contradiction, as well as of architecture's powerlessness qua architecture to effect change.

The debate has certainly moved on. In the post-Reagan, postmodern era, the model for architectural creativity is more and more "big" business. This is both a matter of the rationalization of architectural practice in increasingly indistinguishable corporate offices (SOM, HOK, NBBJ, . . . OMA) and of the way in which the aesthetic supplement itself comes not simply to surrender any idea of its own autonomy but to embrace the criteria and symbols of global capital. This begins as a matter of organization and nomenclature but ultimately defines value: architecture assumes the ethic of business as its highest moral imperative. The rhetoric, however, remains deliriously avant-garde.

It is all always perfectly quantifiable, a matter of market share. In the move to colonize ever-greater markets, no self-respecting corporation can afford to ignore the World Wide Web. Hani Rashid, the Guggenheim's Chief Creative Officer and Chief Technology Officer, describes the motivation behind Guggenheim.com, the expansion of the museum (which has recently acquired its first two works of virtual art) into cyberspace: "There is a notion that art and culture exist sporadically on the Web, and in different places. There's not one location where you have a trusted brand that provides a place where I can call up all of those things." The model for the operation is CNN.com. "They cover a broad range of sports, financial news, etc. The question is: can we create a kind of parallel in the art and culture world?"[10] Rashid celebrates the utility of the Net and the virtual Guggenheim as a memory box, Mnemosyne as a business model, all things for all people. What remains unremarked is the authoritarianism of such hypercentralization of choice.

Erecting their memory palaces in the house of forgetting, though, museums are really just catching up with many artists whose affection for the business model exceeds any other. Indeed, has anyone had a more acute understanding of branding than Andy Warhol, Jeff Koons, Mark Kostabi, Barbara Kruger, or—for that matter—Hans Haacke? Capitalism has increasingly become the subject matter of art, and architecture follows the trailblazers with docility. But as in Vegas, the lines between irony, kitsch, and criticism become monumentally blurred. This is the stage on which the branders dance, the chameleon realm that can always claim a critical position but which unfailingly operates according to the rules of the system.

The crisis of the museum is precisely in the exponential expansion of the artistic territory. Whether the question is of housing the gigantic product of minimalism (Krens's deaccessioning of good paintings to buy a collection of instructions for minimal art is a museological Ponzi—or Panza—scheme), of the endless possibilities of appropriation, or simply of the multiplicity of mechanically reproduced objects that can be designated beautiful, the progressive aestheticization of everything makes the concept irrelevant. The curve of the space required to house the old masters becomes asymptotic, approaching the axis of negligibility as the preponderance of the museum must of necessity be devoted to "contemporary" art, which co-opts every form of material production. Tolerance becomes repression through sheer numeracy, the ultimate indifference to difference.

When the museum goes out of business by going into business, great categories die. It is the same process that Rem applies to urbanism. His formula "World Equals City" is an equation that can lead only to the elimination of the city. Preaching this inevitability is, however, a choice, and not simply an acute bit of teleological thinking about material culture. Removing yet another seam of distinction further reduces choice in the new "empire" of globalization that—for all its vaunted hybridity and flexibility—continues to impose centralized control, uniform values, and the regime of pure profit.

But there are issues here that exceed cynical mockery or crass co-optation. The Venetian Hotel is well known in Vegas for reasons beyond its inclusion of the Guggenheim franchise among the others housed along its interior canals and around its food courts. The singing gondoliers, the waiters at Lutece, the croupiers spinning the roulette wheels, and the dollies doling drinks to the high-rollers are all unorganized: notoriously, the Venetian is a nonunion hotel, much resented in a town in which the unions are strong and effective. Sheldon Adelson—its owner and the client for all this fine architecture—is a legendary foe of unionization, and there are widespread reports of understaffing at the hotel to save wages. Surly service by overworked employees has been a recurring complaint.[11] If there is a politics to architects like Gehry and Koolhaas hawking their brands, it does not devolve on any arcane issues of representation or even, exactly, on the degree of complicity with the corporate powers for whom they provide jestering and high-cultural legitimation. Nor would it be right to call them union busters for making a living from a kind of client from whom architects have always made a living. Nor, for that matter, is Rem wrong to recognize—in the manner of Hardt and Negri—that under the regime of the empire of global capital there is no outside, that there is no approach to the system save from within.

But where *Empire* proposes a politics of resistance, Rem is simply acquiescent, as if nothing were at stake. The advocacy of branding is a sellout in architecture, reducing its meanings to mere advertising, a fine obliviousness to the larger social implications of architectural practice. No amount of bilious insistence that brand is simply the equivalent of culture and its styles of inventing identity can obliterate the transformation. But why rebrand the idea of identity in the first place? Why replace the variety of psychical, cultural, and physical constructs compounded in "identity" with the language of commercial speech? To control it, of course. Branding is just another excuse for power's concentration at the top. The pathetic spectacle of Rem consulting with a number of "leading European intellectuals" to formulate a strategy for the EU flag is precisely as authoritative as the nine out of ten doctors who recommend Preparation H.[12]

This is a very old story: The Platonic critique of rhetoric rings as true for advertising and branding. Socrates' beef with the rhetoricians was that theirs was a practice that could produce persuasion in the absence of belief, a fundamentally mendacious activity. His fear was that the technique could attach itself to any objective, swaying people to act against their own interests. The brand—think of those Benetton ads depicting miserable refugees—is predicated on the same leap. I wear this sweater, therefore I am of good conscience. This is not simply a question of exploiting and cheapening the plight of the oppressed but a distraction from the question of the wretched sweatshop worker producing the brilliantly branded, conscience-saturated goods.

Conflating the defense of brand with the defense of ideas is precisely to deflate the content of the latter. In the era of mechanical reproduction and the death of aura, plagiarism and theft become irrelevant and the meaning of speech arbitrary. The value of the brand can only be defended, therefore, by greater and greater co-optation. Branding is the medium of empire. Free speech? That was *my* idea. I'll see *you* in court. Not long ago, a former employee of OMA sued for what he claimed was the firm's plagiarism of a design he had worked up as his thesis project. Although he lost the case after a lengthy trial, it was a fairly delicious moment and showed the real implications of the fatuous trademarking and copyrighting that have become a whimsical hallmark of Rem's big books. Is he up to the implication? What will he do should Arjun Appadurai—who long ago developed a nuanced version of Rem's mock-copyrighted and nearly empty concept of "scape"—raise an objection to the unacknowledged usurpation? How spirited will his defense of brand be? The real test, though, will be Rem's own first legal claim for infringement—bourgeois morality's ultimate speech-act. Or has the plagiarism suit beaten him to the punch?

Las Vegas and its empire of signage are beautiful the way great advertisements are beautiful. For their technique and pumped-up visuality. For the pleasures of being deceived. For the raising of commercial speech to a shout, deafening as a rock concert. For their impressive powers of self-recreation, the move from rat-pack chic (ironically embodied in the kind of architecture, now blown down, that most closely represents Rem's own formal proclivities) to more postmodern forms of commercial illusion. For, in short, having successfully rebranded themselves as a wholesome nexus of family fun and rump urbanity.

The Koolhaas brand is likewise successful: the man is a master of product placement. As the current architect of choice for cultural institutions self-conscious about their own fading hipness, the agency has just the strategy that you need. If you'll slip into this Sean John tee or this metal box or this transparent dressing room, things will begin to look better. And check out the tomes of market research, branding ideology via sheer weight of irony and statistics. There's charm here. A goof. But in service of what? More junk?

2003

Notes

1. Chuihua Judy Chung, Jeffrey Inaba, Rem Koolhaas, Sze Tsung Leong, eds., *Harvard Design School Guide to Shopping* (Köln: Taschen, 2001), quote on inside of front cover.

2. Joseba Zulaika, "Tough Beauty: Bilbao as Ruin, Architecture, Allegory," in *Iberian Cities*, ed. Joan Ramon Resina (New York and London: Routledge, 2001), 12.

3. "Yesterday, Prada; Tomorrow, the World," *New York Times*, 20 June 2002.

4. Thomas Frank, *One Market under God: Extreme Capitalism, Market Populism, and the End of Economic Democracy* (New York: Doubleday, 2000), 253.

5. Ibid., 254.

6. Ibid., 252.

7. Michael Hardt and Antonio Negri, *Empire* (Cambridge and London: Harvard University Press, 2000), 125.

8. For a truly hilarious peek down the ludicrous rabbit hole of marketing

"theory" and its appropriation of all that is intellectually fashionable, see Stephen Brown, *Post-Modern Marketing 2* (London: Routledge, 1995).

9. Brown, *Post-Modern Marketing 2*, 52.

10. Tom Vanderbilt, "The Culture Shop," *edesign*, March 2002, 46.

11. For a discussion of the role of Sheldon Adelson in the making of the "new" Vegas, see Hal Rothman, *Neon Metropolis* (New York: Routledge, 2002).

12. Chee Pearlman, "First Look: Yesterday, Prada; Tomorrow, the World," *New York Times*, 23 May 2002, F11.

4

Hyphenation Nation: Blurred Forms for a Blurred World

Rick Poynor

Early in the 1990s, I was contacted by a Japanese magazine seeking nominations from people in the design world for a word or concept that would, according to their crystal balls, "define the coming decade." My suggestion was *hybrid*. What a frisson that word then seemed to produce. It suggested a cultural landscape in which old categories of design artificially—and boringly—held apart by outmoded convention would merge in productive and exciting new forms. It contained more than a hint of transgression, as worn-out ways of thinking, making, and acting gave way to liberating creative practices, ideas, and experiences. I was thinking about the old dividing line between art and design, often questioned for sure, but in most real institutional situations still firmly in place. The drive to blur it all seemed everywhere apparent, and postmodernism, still much talked about then, actively encouraged blurring as part of the ongoing meltdown of "high" and "low."

A decade later, the idea of hybridity is now deeply entrenched in the design world. Both the idea and, to some extent, the activity have become commonplace, although that does not stop designers from raving about hybridization as though it were the freshly cut key to a whole new cultural kingdom. In his heavily promoted book *Life Style*, Bruce Mau, Toronto-based graphic designer and sometime collaborator with Rem Koolhaas, rehearses a view of hybridity that few of his designer

34

readers would be inclined to dispute: "Attempting to declare the discrete boundary of any practice, where one ends and another begins, has become arbitrary and artificial," he writes. "On the contrary, the overlap is where the greatest innovation is happening."[1] The two examples that follow this assertion are oddly lightweight, to say the least. Mau mentions the intersection of cinema and digital special effects technologies seen in Gap commercials and *The Matrix*'s action sequences. These media forms are neither one thing nor the other, he proposes, but "a monstrous and beautiful child of the two."[2] Then, to represent the birth of a new kind of culture, Mau jumps to an image adapted from Nietzsche of a chorus in which every singer is a soloist, pushing forward to out-sing the others, pressing against us in the audience, and surrounding us so that we are "embedded" in this singing mass. It is impossible to tell from this passage whether Mau regards this condition as desirable or undesirable, enabling or disabling. Are we, for some reason, supposed to welcome what appears to be an oppressive restriction of our own free movement?

Whether we are talking about image technology, global markets, or digital infrastructure, Mau continues, all of these things demand a "predatory colonization of open space."[3] We have reached the point, he explains, where "Spheres once thought free [from the logic of the market], and even resistant or opposed to it—the museum, the academy, public democratic space—find it ever more difficult to retain autonomy in the face of corporate culture and its sponsorships, educational initiatives, and so-called civic gestures."[4] As small-scale examples of this intrusion, Mau cites print ads above urinals and video ads in elevators, and rightly says these represent just the beginning of a process of "inscription" by commercial imperatives to which there is potentially no end. In the space of just a few hundred words, Mau has moved from an excited declaration that hybridity and the dissolution of boundaries are generating our most significant cultural innovations to an almost neutral-sounding acknowledgment that practically nowhere, apart from a few unspoiled bits of nature, is free from "hostile takeover" by market forces. The direction of his argument implies a link between the two, but he does not acknowledge it outright, and this reluctance to make and act on the connection is symptomatic of the bind in which many designers now find themselves.

The market itself shows no such hesitation to engineer and exploit the link of capitalism and culture. Business literature provides an abundance of evidence that cultural ideas that might have seemed avant-garde and progressive in *artistic* circles ten or fifteen years ago are now routine shoptalk in *business* circles. *Funky Business* by Jonas Ridderstråle and Kjell Nordström, a pair of Swedish PhDs who brandish their hairless heads as a hip personal trademark, is an international bestseller translated, at last count, into nineteen languages. King of the corporate gurus Tom Peters, for one, says, in a cover blurb, that they offer a "defiantly funky perspective on the new world order" and that this new world order is founded on the twin principles, interminably reiterated, of continuous change and exhilarating uncertainty. According to Ridderstråle and Nordström, we live in a "blurred society" in which conventional divides and structures, once used to sort experience into neat categories, are falling into disarray: industries and relationships between companies are blurring, products and services are blurring, and so is the traditional distinction between leisure and work. "Everywhere we look, we see blur—East-West, Men-Women, Structure-Process, Right-Wrong."[5] For entrepreneurial individuals and organizations, they argue, these changes are not mysterious or threatening, and they do not spell chaos; they should instead be grasped as opportunities for restructuring and innovation.

The funky Swedes offer a vision of the future in which we inhabit a cut-and-paste "hyphe-nation" where the solution to having more than enough of what already exists is to create a never-ending stream of brand-new things by combining old things in novel ways—"the weirder the combination," they exult, "the more unique the result."[6] They list some recent hyphenations: edu-tainment, info-tainment, distance-learning, psycho-linguistics, bio-tech, corporate-university. As they see it, variation has the potential to breed ever more variation as gleaming new hyphenates are deliriously spliced together in a chain of multiplication that is potentially limitless, so long as "value" is added in the process. "At the same time," they caution, "it needs to be difficult for the consumer to unbundle the offering. Because if the customer can easily separate the things that have been combined, he or she can use increasingly perfected markets to get one or all of these items from someone else."[7]

While it was doubtless not their intention, Ridderstråle and Nordström have succinctly expressed the problem faced by many contributors to culture today and, perhaps above all, by designers. The question is precisely how it might be possible to "unbundle the offering." In the relationship of business and culture, the process of blurring, hyphenation, hybridization—call it what you will—is so far advanced that it is easy to take it for granted and cease to question what might have been lost on the way. All the rhetoric focuses relentlessly on what is supposedly gained. Merely to use the word "innovation" as a rallying cry, as Mau does, as the business-friendly Swedes do, is to suggest developments that cannot be gainsaid, wealth-generating outcomes that, according to the logic of the market, are inherently desirable, irrespective of their ulterior meanings or effects.

By the end of the 1990s, the feeling that there was almost no resisting these changes ran deep, and this being the case, the only sensible response was to collude. In December 1999, an issue of *Utne Reader* with the cover story "The Great American Sellout" noted that "The rewards are now so high it's often seen as foolish, even pathological, to resist."[8] A British novelist, writing in the style magazine *Dazed & Confused,* set out the new priorities for herself and her friends: "Fuck all that spiritual bullshit about mental growth and exploration and experience, we wanted the goods. The hardware. Cash, clothes, cars, luxury apartments."[9] A London design journalist, Alice Rawsthorn, now director of the city's Design Museum, phrased the issue more delicately, though just as materialistically, in promotional copy for the fashion company Caterpillar. It took eight years, she notes, between Jack Kerouac setting off on the road and his appearance in *Playboy*'s "Beat" issue, while hot artist Tracey Emin made it on to billboards for Bombay Sapphire gin in a matter of months and was handsomely recompensed for it. "Maybe the commercialization thing we get so hung up on these days comes down to just that," Rawsthorn offers. "If everything's now up for grabs, then are you master or servant of your own life's commodification?"[10] Last year, the style magazine *Sleazenation* provided one possible answer with what some might have regarded as a truly innovative cover concept: "Absolut(e) sell out." On the back cover, it ran an Absolut ad, "Absolut Morph"—the new product blends vodka and citrus flavors, hyphenation and mutability being once again the visual theme—while the front showed a model sporting covetable items by Yves Saint Laurent, Gucci, and Chanel, with prices and supplier details attached. "To a certain extent we are all sell-outs now," the editor confessed in a note. "Any individual or organization attempting to disseminate their cultural message will find that corporate involvement—i.e. cash—is becoming increasingly necessary to facilitate this. This is not necessarily a good thing or a bad thing. It is also inevitable."[11] No argument about its inevitability from the business side: A recent issue of *Fast Company* proposed that fringe ideas generated by social and artistic deviants are the very stuff of mass markets. The magazine's advice? "Sell out! Sure, it lacks integrity, but the benefits can be pretty nice."[12]

Once we dissolve the old boundary lines and concede the territory to corporate forces, it is extremely difficult to win it back. From our compromised position embedded in the new hyphenated reality in which the culture-business depends on the drip-drip-drip of corporate largesse, it becomes hard to imagine that there could be any other way of doing things, especially if this is the only reality we have known. Any misgivings can be waved aside with the claim that this state of affairs is now simply inevitable, so we might as well grab the benefits with both hands, and any criticism can be rejected as a point of view that naively fails to understand the financial expediency of culture's pact with commerce. When Morgan Stanley, sponsor of "Surrealism: Desire Unbound" at Tate Modern in London, draws a parallel between the way the surrealists "threw back the boundaries of conventional art by challenging conventional thinking" and its own history of "challenging traditional thinking to help our clients raise their financial aspirations," such a comparison has long since ceased to strike some of us as the slightest bit absurd.[13]

Since design is by its nature heavily dependent on commercial patronage, its practitioners have no great incentive to analyze the relationship. Attempts to encourage designers to do so are highly instructive. In 1999, I became involved in a project initiated by *Adbusters*, the Canadian anticorporate magazine, to redraft and relaunch a design manifesto called *First Things First* (FTF), originally published in London in 1964. The rewritten document, *First Things First 2000*, signed by thirty-three visual communicators and a smattering of critics, appeared in several North American magazines, received plenty of coverage, and can be read at *Adbusters'* Web site, so I shall not attempt to outline its contents at any length here.[14] Aimed at communication designers, the four-hundred-word text argues that today most of designers' talent and effort is directed toward the advertising, marketing, and promotion of consumer products and services, while less commercial areas of design, such as social marketing campaigns, educational tools, charitable causes, and information design projects, receive much less attention. The manifesto proposes instead a "reversal of priorities in favor of more useful, lasting, and democratic forms of communication."

Of course the chances of such a reversal, desirable as it might be,

Adbusters corporate flag. www.adbusters.org.

Adbusters barcode flag. www.adbusters.org.

were never better than remote, but it is sometimes necessary to over-state a case even to begin to make it, and the manifesto's idealism certainly caught many designers' attention and infuriated more than a few. The text's central purpose was to ask design professionals to think about their own position and priorities and, if they were unhappy with this position, to do something about it. Its primary audience was always likely to be younger designers and design students still forming their views, and this proved to be the case. For many older, established designers, FTF's relatively modest proposal, even its mere existence, was hugely presumptuous. They looked at the manifesto's list of com-mercial products (dog biscuits, hair gel, credit cards, sneakers, recrea-tional vehicles, and so on), recognized that this was indeed the kind of promotional design work on which they lavished their time, skill, and imagination, and rejected FTF out of hand. Moreover, the text arrived at a moment—shortly before the Seattle WTO protest and the publication of Naomi Klein's *No Logo: Taking Aim at the Brand Bullies*—when there were no highly visible public signs of disaffection with the decade's triumphalist capitalism. To many, it looked like an inexplicable throwback to some rightly defunct way of thinking, and even if it did not, the fundamentally political questions it posed were always going to unnerve a profession that proceeds, all too often, as though politics did not exist.

One question raised by some of the manifesto's critics is the extent to which FTF is urging designers to opt out of commercial work and abandon this realm to the hacks, thus ensuring that standards are de-based even further. The manifesto does not seek to prohibit commer-cial work or ask designers to stop doing it entirely. It simply suggests that the amount of attention this area receives is disproportionate and that being on the receiving end of an unceasing barrage of commercial communication, produced in part by designers, is bound to have an effect, probably detrimental, on the way we see the world. This may seem blindingly obvious, but designers deeply embedded in the com-mercial sphere, who take its priorities and dominance for granted, are often reluctant to address the point. There *is* perhaps an argument now for refusing to engage on any level other than the critical with the commercial world, and some graphic designers do take this course, though clearly, for those involved in larger-scale, three-dimensional design and architecture, it will be an even more difficult path.

In a fascinating recent polemic, *The Twilight of American Culture,* social critic Morris Berman takes a scathing look at the United States today and concludes that despite the vigor and vitality of contemporary commercial culture, the nation is locked into a pattern of decline—evinced by social inequality, loss of entitlements, decreasing intellectual abilities, and spiritual death—which it is powerless to prevent. This decline will play itself out regardless, and the outcome will not be known until we are no longer around. What can be done then, here and now, to ensure that when the time finally comes, enlightened values still survive so that a more receptive society can make use of them again to revivify itself? Berman's answer is a strategy inspired by what happened to classical knowledge during the Dark Ages when manuscripts were faithfully copied and preserved in the monasteries by monks who almost certainly did not understand their contents. When the moment for cultural revival came in the twelfth century, the knowledge was there to be used. Berman calls his proposal "the monastic option," and the essence of the idea is that people who feel they do not fit in with consumer society's prevailing values find ways of practicing at a local level—and so keeping alive—the values they hold dear. He stresses the individualistic nature of this strategy, cautions against the constant dangers of institutionalization and co-optation by commerce, and rejects the notion of a life based on kitsch, consumerism, profit, fame, and self-promotion. Among his examples are *Adbusters,* David Barsamian's "Alternative Radio" program on National Public Radio, and violinist Olga Bloom's Bargemusic, which presents chamber music in a wood-paneled concert hall in a converted coffee barge floating off Brooklyn. Berman accepts the fact that we have no way of knowing how the future will turn out and that his idea might be no more than wishful thinking. Yet, as he reasonably observes, "If we make *no* attempt to preserve the best in our culture, we can rest assured that the possibility of cultural renewal is pretty much ruled out."[15]

Even if they agree with this conclusion, most designers will probably wish to find a way of collaborating with commercial forces. They frequently talk about "changing things from the inside," but to do this, if it is possible at all, will require a clarity of political analysis, a strength of critical purpose, and a tactical readiness to accept the fact that most interventions are likely to be short-lived, while the fundamental nature of the political and economic system remains intact. Few seem to possess these tools in practice, and even those who

No Shop store, London. www.adbusters.org.

come closest have drawn legitimate criticism. The late Tibor Kalman, starting from the premise that "Our culture is corporate culture," proposes a "modest solution" in his book *Perverse Optimist*: "Find the cracks in the wall." In other words, hook up with entrepreneurs crazy enough to allow you to use their money to change the world.[16] Kalman's most sustained attempt to do this was with Benetton, for whom he conceived and edited thirteen issues of *Colors* magazine. Thomas Frank, writing in *Artforum*, was perhaps the only commentator to point out the naïveté of Kalman's political position, which posed no fundamental challenge to the knitwear giant.[17] In *Life Style*, Mau's opening gambit is to distance himself from culture jammers (such as *Adbusters*, presumably), who do at least make it clear where they stand with their anticorporate rhetoric and actions. Mau's definition of engagement with the conditions of our time, or what he calls the "global image economy," apparently requires that judgment be postponed "while we search for an exit."[18] If this sounds unhelpfully hazy, much of what Mau has to say in the book about his practice seems simultaneously oracular and opaque, a warning sign that he wants to have it both ways, to reap the professional rewards of working for the "regime of the logo and its image" (Mau's words) while affecting to critique it—a contradiction pointed out in reviews by both Mark Kingwell and Hal Foster.[19]

One senses here the influence of Mau's colleague Rem Koolhaas, an architect and observer for whom the suspension of judgment has become an operational strategy. The problem, as always, is how to "unbundle the offering" as these culture-business hybrids become increasingly imaginative, persuasive, and compelling. Dan Weiden, founder and CEO of Weiden+Kennedy, Nike's advertising agency for the past twenty years, recently renovated a ninety-year-old landmark building in Portland, Oregon's downtown Pearl District. Then, in a canny move, he invited the Portland Institute of Contemporary Art, a fledgling arts organization with a reputation for promoting edgy young artists, to become a tenant. Weiden was already a PICA board member, and he hoped that the presence of artists would help reenergize the agency's creative atmosphere by blurring the boundaries imposed by traditional conceptions of advertising and by opening up fresh ways of communicating.

"It's not altruism—it's an investment," he told *Fast Company*. "And in some ways, it's extremely selfish. The bet is that there will be concrete rewards and spiritual rewards for us and for our clients, who hire us to talk to people in a way that's both meaningful and surprising."[20] It is easy to see the appeal for a struggling arts institution of finding a home in such a spectacular space (designed by Brad Cloepfil and his firm Allied Works Architecture, Inc.), just as it takes no great leap of imagination to grasp what a pleasure it would be for agency personnel to work in such an ambience. Yet the relationship is troubling because it crystallizes a systemic truth about the relative power of advertising and a local arts organization, as the larger of the two entities literally ingests and displays the smaller, weaker one for its own purposes. The implication for both advertising and art, and for people in the community who visit PICA in this space, is that the boundaries are now fully permeable and that art and advertising are not so different in essence—it is all just "creativity" and "communication." The process of boundary erosion is happening everywhere, and PICA's presence within W+K only confirms its normality.

At Prada's "Epicenter" store on Prince Street and Broadway in Manhattan, this erosion is even more subtly embodied. The hybridization

OMA/Rem Koolhaas, exterior of Prada, New York City, 2002. Photograph copyright Frank Oudeman.

of culture and commerce has been so artfully achieved here that walking around the 24,500-square-foot space designed by Rem Koolhaas and OMA, one doesn't experience the queasy sensation of being an interloper that snooty fashion shops so often induce. The underlying sales function is giddily subsumed into something much more loosely defined. With its half-hidden video screens in all shapes and sizes, its huge cylindrical glass-sided elevator, and its vast wall of anti-avant-garde wallpaper, it is more like the latest thing in funky, high-tech arts centers than a shop. If the Italian fashion company means to convey the impression that its Epicenter store is, at least in part, a public space, then it succeeds; on Saturdays the place is reportedly thronged with people who have dropped by to hang out and gawk. Prada's plan is to stage public performances in the auditorium sculpted from a ravishing sweep of zebrawood. "In a world where everything is shopping . . . and shopping is everything . . . what is luxury?" asks Koolhaas in Prada's book about the project. "Luxury is NOT shopping." Once the consumer's attention has been captured by Prada, he says, it can be generously handed back to her. He even drops a mysterious hint about eventually returning "the public back to the public."[21]

This and other statements by Koolhaas, as in Mau's attempt to locate the exit, suggest that we shall one day emerge from the hyphenation nation. How it will happen, they don't say. How projects that serve commercial efforts are going to bring it about, they also don't say. I met Koolhaas recently in Rotterdam and asked him whether he enjoyed shopping. He gave an indirect, inconclusive reply; perhaps his answer would have revealed too much. I asked him about his "Junkspace" essay, a bleak vision of entire cities blurring and hyphenating to form the ultimate, undifferentiated hybrid-space, a monotonous, textureless, urban black hole.[22] Here, finally, he appears—but perhaps it is no more than appears—to be making a judgment. In person, though, he is more circumspect. "This situation, which has gotten slightly out of hand, will somehow be, not so much corrected, but followed by something that finds new forms of interest," he says. This is scrupulously noncommittal. I wish I could say that it helps. Maybe the time has come to insist on the validity of some of our earlier categories and distinctions—between art and non-art, between instrumental work and work undertaken for its own sake. Operating without them is about as effective, as a method of resistance, as looking for a pathway in a fog.

2003

Notes

1. Bruce Mau, *Life Style* (London: Phaidon Press, 2000), 41–43.

2. Ibid., 43.

3. Ibid., 45.

4. Ibid.

5. Jonas Ridderstråle and Kjell Nordström, *Funky Business: Talent Makes Capital Dance* (London and New York: Pearson Education, 2002; first published 2000), 135.

6. Ibid., 143.

7. Ibid., 144.

8. Jeremiah Creedon, "Seller's Market," *Utne Reader,* December 1999, 52.

9. Bidisha [sic], "Show Me the Money," *Dazed & Confused,* October 2000, unpaginated.

10. Alice Rawsthorn in *We Shape the Things We Build, Thereafter They Shape Us,* Caterpillar brochure, 1999, unpaginated.

11. Steve Slocombe, "It's a Sell-Out," *Sleazenation,* October 2001, 5.

12. Ryan Mathews and Watts Wacker, "Deviants, Inc.," *Fast Company,* March 2002, 76.

13. "Sponsor's Foreword," *Surrealism: Desire Unbound,* ed. Jennifer Mundy (London: Tate Publishing, 2001), 6.

14. Both versions of the *First Things First* manifesto are at www.adbusters .org.

15. Morris Berman, *The Twilight of American Culture* (London: Duckworth, 2000), 99.

16. Tibor Kalman, "Fuck Committees (I Believe in Lunatics)," in *Tibor Kalman: Perverse Optimist,* ed. Peter Hall and Michael Bierut (New York: Princeton Architectural Press, 1998), unpaginated.

17. Thomas Frank, "Half Empty," *Artforum,* February 1999, 26–28.

18. Mau, *Life Style,* 39.

19. See Mark Kingwell, "Interior Decoration: Politics as Lifestyle Accessory," *Harper's Magazine,* June 2001, 72–75; and Hal Foster, "Hey, That's Me," *London Review of Books,* 5 April 2001, 13–14.

20. Quoted in Rob Lieber, "Creative Space," *Fast Company,* January 2001, 142.

21. Rem Koolhaas, Miuccia Prada, and Patrizio Bertelli, *Projects for Prada Part 1* (Milan: Fondazione Prada Edizioni, 2001), unpaginated.

22. Rem Koolhaas, "Junkspace," in *Harvard Design School Guide to Shopping,* ed. Chuihua Judy Chung, Jeffrey Inaba, Rem Koolhaas, and Sze Tsung Leong (Köln: Taschen, 2001), 408–21.

5

Architecture for Sale(s):
An Unabashed Apologia

Kevin Ervin Kelley

Moralism, Buying, and Selling

Some think that buying things you don't "need" is immoral, but all of us do it, and if we were honest, we would admit that it's harmless and we enjoy it. In Asia, the people I have encountered don't think so puritanically—even Buddhist monks welcome the pleasures of shopping in the markets. We designers are not really producing what people need; we are producing what they *want*. Our economy is based on creating those wants. In my firm, which designs to sell things, we study not only how people behave in stores but also anthropology, sociology, psychology, demography, and pop culture to understand what they want.[1] When we help satisfy their wants, we give them moments of pleasure. Designers can be proud when they do that.

The only selling or retailing that is immoral is that which either lies about its product or that harms people in the long run. Selling lottery tickets is not in itself immoral, despite the low odds of customers' winning. But encouraging people who cannot afford lottery tickets to buy them often is immoral, just as it is immoral for someone in an impoverished family to buy them often. Yet a poor person buying an occasional lottery ticket is buying a dream as much as is a rich person buying a yacht. A lot of architects think, as I once did, that business is nothing but greed. But we don't understand it. Most businesspeople are proud of what they sell and believe it will improve people's lives—at the very least by giving them pleasure.

Some may argue that much if not most of retailing takes advantage of people's weaknesses: their need to delude themselves that if they have this or that product, they will be more attractive, intelligent, secure, youthful, cool, loved, and so on. The ultimate result of shopping, in this argument, is disappointment, disillusion, even depression. My response is that people will have such delusions whether or not they are shopping and that the pleasures of positive fantasy outweigh the pains of a letdown to "realism." Moralists decrying shopping are as tiresome and crabby as those who argue that being entertained by mindless action movies weakens our "character."

Furthermore, retailing provides us with another "good" that is rare or absent from the rest of our lives: places to gather enjoyably with other people. Look at, for instance, Starbucks and Borders bookstores; if we don't have gazebos on town greens, we do have lounge chairs in stores like these. Many places where the public now gathers for shopping are also scenes of pleasant social activities and events, from musical and theatrical performances to encounters with friends.

Most of us are familiar with the best-selling business books with clever titles about swimming with sharks and seven effective habits, but these are more like self-help manuals than serious studies. Formulaic and simplistic, they give business a bad rap. The best of business writing—by, for instance, Theodore Levitt, Michael Porter, Philip Kotler, Al Ries, Jack Trout, and David Ogilvy—is worthy of attention from all professionals and is as thoughtful, sociological, political, and consequential as good architecture.[2]

Hypocritical "Superiority" to Retailing

We architects, trained to think of ourselves as commissioned artists, often shun architecture that helps companies sell. The mere discussion of architecture's role in sales rubs the tradition-groomed hair of architects the wrong way. We associate retailers with snake oil salesmen and pretend to be uninvolved in the "evils" of consumerism. While we may not be as materialistic as our neighbors, we refuse to accept the fact that retailing is a major and unavoidable part of our lives and environment. All of us, including high-art architects, are consumers;

we buy not only groceries, gas, and clothes but also museum tickets, books, magazines, education, and even opportunities to commune with nature. We have been conditioned to believe that retailing is a dishonest, manipulative practice that preys on unsuspecting victims and corrupts our art. A respected academic recently told one of my students that if he weren't careful, he might end up designing Wal-Marts. While I am not a fan of Wal-Mart, I find it very telling that we have written off the world's largest corporation.

When my partner and I started a design firm in 1992, we wanted to accept American culture on its own terms, to confirm people's enjoyment in going to places like Rainforest Cafe, Disney World, and Las Vegas. Although I find Las Vegas casinos obnoxious and garish, a lot of people have very good times in them. Something's happening. And we can choose to deny it or think that we are looking at a sham . . . or we can look at it openly. When I began to try to understand what Americans really enjoy, I started taking control of my professional life. My partner and I did not want to call our work "architecture," because many people were confused into thinking it was *only* architecture, so we called ourselves Shook Design Group. After many years of competing against ad agencies, accounting firms, and business consultants, I learned that even the word *design* hurt our ability to get in the right doors and gain respect in the business world. Business clients have been conditioned to believe that "designers" will always give away ideas for free. We have changed our firm name again to shed the word *design* . . . more on that later.

The Omnipresence of Retailing

Retailing has become significantly more present in more disparate environments than it was a decade or two ago. Consider airlines. Passengers buy products from catalogs in seat pockets. What once was a limited retail channel has become a booming market. Shopping provides the traveler with a means of reducing the stress, aggravation, boredom, and fear of flying. While some may see back-of-the-seat marketing as a plot by rapacious corporations to push products on us at one of our weakest and most captive moments, I argue just the opposite. People *enjoy* the experience of buying, sometimes more than having the products themselves, because the moment of buying is one of enthusiastic fantasy and escape (which, in this case, takes our minds off the anxieties of flying).

Airport terminals have become major retail outlets. Fifteen years ago, going to the airport was like stopping at a roadside rest area, with vending machines and (if you were lucky) some rotating hot dogs. Every major metropolitan airport in America now has a wide range of restaurants such as Chili's, California Pizza Kitchen, and Cheers. After finishing our meals, we can stroll down the retail promenade and buy watches from Fossil, jeans from Gap, leather jackets from Wilson's, pens from Mont Blanc, even shoes from Johnston & Murphy. (The Johnston & Murphy outlet in the Philadelphia airport is one of the top grossing stores in the shoe store chain, selling $700 per square foot.)[3] Our airports are no longer boring and bland.

Look at any major institution—museums, zoos, parks, universities, stadiums, even churches—and you will see the growing presence of retail. We are inviting, encouraging, and *demanding* retailers to be more involved in our lives. The first thing that urban planners now think about for downtown revitalization is stores; they use retail and restaurants to create movement, activity, and renewed energy on the street, which will attract investors, home owners, and other kinds of businesses. Churches sell day-care and fitness services; corporate buildings have gift shops, cafeterias, retail stores, and recreation centers, as well as services like dry cleaning and auto maintenance. Hospitals sell sports medicine, wellness education, alternative practices, and cosmetics. Long considered the holdout, even municipalities are beginning to embrace consumerism, hiring branding firms to create logos and other images that will attract new people and businesses.

Retail Planning and Design as a Big Opportunity for Architects

Whether you are going to the mall, to church, or to the library, each venue has a specific exchange value that architects can either embrace or ignore. We architects should be leading the way, instead of allowing allied professions like graphic, industrial, and technology designers to claim and own the embodiment of this value. If we continue to avoid marketing in the built environment, it will be at our peril.

To date, retailing strategy has been left primarily to advertisers, marketers, accounting firms, banks, stockbrokers, and a few design firms. Ironically, the nondesigners on this list are more conscious of the need for strong design in what they produce than is the average architect. During the 1950s and 1960s, advertisers and psychologists started teaming up to create the popular and controversial field of motivational research. The most famous critic of this theory was Vance Packard, who in 1957 wrote in the best-selling *Hidden Persuaders* that "large scale efforts are being made, often with impressive success, to channel our thinking habits, our purchasing decisions, and our thought process. . . . The result is that many of us are being influenced and manipulated, far more than we realize, in the patterns of our everyday lives."[4] Packard's major target was infamous ad man and psychologist Ernest Dichter. Dichter was the director of the Institute for Motivational Research (founded in 1946) and was credited with the brilliant marketing strategies for Barbie, Exxon, Betty Crocker, and other successes. Dichter defined motivational research as "qualitative research designed to uncover the consumer's subconscious or hidden motivations that determine purchase behavior."[5] The intent of motivational research was to shift marketers' attention to thoughts and emotions. While Packard and Dichter have been criticized for exaggerating the power of subliminal messages in advertising, their theories sparked a revolution in the study of the relationship between emotions and purchasing. This revolution has now led us to "lifestyle marketing" (see below).

Fifty-six years after the founding of the Institute for Motivational Research, advertising and marketing agencies are acquiring (and considering acquiring) architecture firms because they need them to provide environments that they now see profoundly affect consumer perception and behavior.[6] Until we architects begin to think like capitalists, these agencies will continue to take work we could have. For them design is a means to an end, not an end in itself. Nevertheless, even instrumental design can be appreciated *as* design: we all enjoy well-crafted, witty, and beautiful ads. (And plenty of design for its own sake is still around to be appreciated: it is called art.) Architects who embrace retailing are best organized as "integrated design services firms" providing not only design expertise but also strategic business consulting, branding, marketing, and sometimes even advertising. To design well, architects need to do these other activities well.

Successful retailers are switching from product marketing to "lifestyle marketing." Lifestyle marketing reaches far beyond the consumer's "needs" to tap into his or her deepest longings. Instead of dividing consumers into demographic groups, lifestyle marketing categorizes them into attitudinal segments that better reflect their core values. Those core values center on primal desires: to acquire, belong, interact, be healthy, have prestige, feel secure, and so on. The group of consumers that longs to feel "cool" (or sexy or macho or petite or smart or . . .) cuts across class, gender, racial, and ethnic divides. Pottery Barn and Martha Stewart are two examples of lifestyle (not product) brands.

Appealing to consumers' core values can be achieved through a display that acts as a surrogate for the brand and merchandises lifestyles by "vignetting." Vignetting is mocking up a desirable scene with all the right props (merchandise). Each season Pottery Barn "re-merchandises" its windows with vignettes that stage things like the perfect summer picnic party, Christmas, Thanksgiving. . . . The store is selling certain *experiences* by selling the props for those experiences: not just furniture but also pillows, linens, picture frames, flatware, candles, cookbooks, and mood music. The shopper's fantasy of living better has become more important than the actual product.

Before architects can begin the pre-design process, we must first understand our clients within the context of their industries, corporate cultures, brands, and most of all, consumers' minds. What is the client's core competency, and how can it be matched with opportunities in the marketplace? Retailers now understand that to be competitive they must make their sales venues extensions of their brand images and promises. Consumers want to immerse themselves in three-dimensional experiences. As architects, we are in the best of all positions to help retailers create branding environments, but we will first have to incorporate broader knowledge and skills into our practice with the help of psychology, sociology, anthropology, advertising, and market positioning.

Rather than relying on pre-design and programming, my firm employs a more extensive (and profitable) process that starts with researching the client, the desired consumer's characteristics and aspirations, as well as relevant popular culture and societal cues (such as Britney Spears and Shania Twain exposing their belly buttons, empty nesters moving into cities, suburban white kids emulating urban rappers). We look for opportunities to observe consumers in similar environments and similar purchasing situations. We then begin to do inner-life profiling of the consumers based on field observations that may yield data about the kind of car they drive, the way they wear their hair, the kind of shoes they wear, and the music they listen to, as well as whether they seem happy or sad, lethargic or excited while in certain stores. We are not conducting scientific surveys. Our interest is to understand motivations that are not easily articulated. We jokingly state that if we can see inside a consumer group's medicine cabinet, refrigerator, and closets, we can predict almost all of its purchasing habits. Once we understand deeper motivations, we explore design solutions. We create "two-second icons"—images to be associated with the products, the essences of which can be perceived in the key two seconds in which shoppers decide whether to pay more attention— that trigger consumers' emotive valuations. The two-second icon becomes the basis for all other design, becomes the brand logo.

Since its inception, our firm has not done speculative work. We have sold ideas to people who needed and would pay for them. One of the most masochistic things designers can do is give their time for free. Our major emphasis should *not* be on negotiating and selling construction documents. We ought to sell our ideas and give away construction documents. Ideas are our commodity. "You'll be paid 8 to 10 percent of construction costs" is a hideous statement. Ideas are not related to square footage; they should be sold based on their ultimate value to the client. A big idea merits a big check.

Designing Perceptions

After a decade of studying consumers in retail environments, I saw more clearly that people do not respond to the world as it is or how we, as designers, want it to be but to their perceptions of it. Calling what our firm does "architecture" was quite confusing for all involved, so we redefined our service as "Perception Design"—we help prompt consumers to buy through environmental "signaling" that influences their perceptions. In a sense, we are designing the consumers themselves. Brand cueing takes place in the built elements but also the menu, uniforms, logo, aromas, and music, plus sensations, and, most importantly, emotions. Most architects are surprised that our firm generally will not take on a project unless we are involved in evaluating all elements of the brand. We changed the firm's name to the single word *Shook* with the tag line "It's All Consuming." We thus tell people that we eagerly embrace consumerism.

Perception, our main concern, is an interpretation of sensory stimuli colored chiefly by memory and experience, not the "facts." The chefs who understand how to shape perception (not the best chefs) have the best restaurants. Restaurant critics may tell you that the only things that matter are the quality of food, the ambience, and the service. But what matters is actually the perception of those things—and these perceptions vary with different kinds of people. Some think a huge tender steak makes a meal great; others think it is two ounces of artfully arranged organic greens. The best restaurants are figuring out who you are, then shaping your perceptions to match your desires.

When you buy a product based on seeing its surrogate—a picture or a film of what having the product will be like—the "reality" of the product is unimportant. You need the surrogate. We can put a really nice hat, with stars at the top, on some anonymous model and make everybody believe he is a chef. But the second you let people who want to sell you something be "natural," potential buyers do not know whether to believe them. They need surrogates to build this credibility. You must reach consumers in a dramatic, compelling way. This is where our training as designers comes into play. Look at a sneaker with no logo on it; it is just rubber and plastic, boring. Take the same sneaker, put on a Swoosh, and its value quadruples. Things are not logical in retail. People decide on the cleanliness of a restaurant according to the cleanliness of its bathroom. Decoding these kinds of things is what designers should include in their practices.

Images are strategic weapons in our society. We pick our politicians based on their images. We do not choose them because of their IQs, knowledge, or school attendance. We do not even care about their criminal records. More often than not, their images are fabricated, so the consumer has gotten smart enough to wonder about the integrity of the image. The making of images thus has to get more and more sophisticated. The saddest thing about our last presidential election was that neither candidate had the ability to "convene" us by making himself a distinctive brand. The issues debated were not important enough to us. Branding pulls us into a place to which we respond. Branding creates trust.

Architects have not been driving home the fact that we are designers of perception through image making. We want to think that images are too shallow and that architecture plumbs deeper matters: tectonics, space, habitability, art, and so on. But in the days after the agricultural society, the manufacturing society, and even the information society, we have come to the era of images, and it is ours to shape.

Images can be effective and helpful or ineffective and useless; images save us time when we are as absurdly busy as we are.

One of our firm's designs was for the grocery store chain Harris Teeter. We referred to our design as a store on steroids. A grocery store is a square box with no windows. How can you make that exciting? We deployed environmental cues that communicated value, quality, customization, and fun. Every designed element of the store—the floor, the ceiling, the wall murals, the signage, and so on—was tested in focus groups. Consumers' reactions to the physical environment are often surprising: we found that they believe exposed ceilings and concrete floors (as opposed to drop ceilings and VCT tile) communicate that the products are cheaper (usually they are not). We found that murals and chalkboards boosted the perception of quality, authority, and freshness in certain categories (milk, meat, coffee, etc.), and sales went way up. Not all of this information can be gathered in focus groups. Most intelligent consumers would argue that murals, chalkboards, and so on have no impact on their buying habits, but we found that when we took down the meat department mural, sales went down. Most of what motivates consumers is way below the surface of their consciousness. Designing successful retail requires diving under that surface. Many would say that we manipulate consumers; we think that we are helping stores get credit (purchases) for the things they do well.

A Case in Point

Over three years, our firm provided the brand strategy and design for a Philadelphia-based food chain, Genuardi's Family Markets—a third-generation, family-run business of about twenty-eight stores. Although Genuardi's was the best-liked grocery chain in Philadelphia, it was experiencing strong competition from bargain stores and the high-end, top-quality Zagara's.

Prior to our involvement, an accounting and strategy consulting firm recommended to Genuardi's that they buy Zagara's. After the purchase, the consultants developed a plan for merging Zagara's and Genuardi's cultures and brands. Not long after they introduced this plan, the chain experienced significant consumer dissatisfaction, weaker sales, and increased internal fighting. Business consultants exacerbated these problems, and Genuardi's decided to hire us.

When we studied the two brands as they had been prior to merging, we found that they had equal status in the minds of their consumers for completely different reasons. We distilled these findings into two "brand vision" charts that outlined a variety of factors—a profile of their best customers and their emotional bonds with the stores, and what each store's brand "promise" had been. We then developed a strategy not to integrate but again to distinguish the stores so the two brands and cultures could operate differently but with the common goal of capturing the broadest range of consumers.

Each of a supermarket's departments—dry goods, perishables, and prepared foods—has different profit margins. Products manufactured, branded, and labeled by outside vendors, such as General Mills, have slim profit margins because the supermarket is acting as a middleman. The profitability of prepared foods can be much greater, especially if they are private label brands that enhance the overall image of the chain and encourage customer loyalty. Our client sought to enhance its identity and increase profits by creating a brand for its prepared foods department as well as sub-brands for about seventy-five products in that department.

Working closely with the client's branding team, our firm began to decode the places where good food for good value comes from, including Mom's kitchen, farms and farmers' markets, certain restaurants, fast-food venues, food courts, and grocery stores. We knew that to be successful, the private label brands and the prepared foods department would have to overcome the perception that grocery stores are for from-scratch ingredients only, that they do not have good prepared foods, and that they are inconvenient.

The images we used needed to evoke quality, freshness, reliability, and healthy indulgence, as well as convenience and value. Architecture alone was not going to accomplish this, so our team included not only a principal-in-charge, a project architect, and two interior designers but also a brand manager, a graphic designer, and an environmental graphic designer. We worked with our client's CEO, COO, and vice presidents of marketing and "acquisition integration," as well as with the directors of operations, food service, and merchandising services. Together we identified the brand of the chain, created a brand "position" among its competitors, and closely studied the brand audiences. The result was a "store within a store" with a separate name and entrance. This helped the supermarket distinguish the prepared food area from the grocery store. Consumers perceived its separate entrance and checkout as convenient, and its European layout and finishes as cues for "good food."

The client's branding team came up with the name "The Kitchen," and we responded by designing its logo using anthropomorphic figures (consumers love anthropomorphic figures). The Kitchen logo was applied to packaging for foods cooked in the store—bakery and deli items, coffee, and pizza. The chain had acquired a bakery

Sunset Mills Artisan Breads logo. Copyright Kevin Kelley/Shook Kelley.

called Sunset, so we created a separate label for their line of "artisan breads" called Sunset Mills. Other Sunset Mills' products included specially packaged olive oil and product information/nutrition cards.

In the Kitchen's meat section, two more label brands helped create a perception of quality. For the premium "all-natural" beef, we created the brand name "Dakota Reserve," and for other meats—chicken, pork, turkey, and ground beef—the name "Up Country." None of these

View of "Sea Fresh" Department, Harris Teeter Supermarket. Copyright Kevin Kelley/Shook Kelley.

meats actually changed, but meat sales rose by 15 to 16 percent. The bread packaging and bread cart we designed form an environment in which shoppers were meant to be immersed in an aura of Old World craftsmanship. The Kitchen immediately exceeded sales of similar product groupings in the chain's other stores by an average of 15 percent.

These results demonstrate how architectural firms can increase their clients' profitability by branching out into related design disciplines. But there are many more opportunities for architects in retailing. After 9/11, President Bush and Mayor Giuliani encouraged us to go shopping to help strengthen America. While I find this message scary and naive, it demonstrates how vital retail is to our economy. Not all retail is good—at times retailers find our neuroses more profitable than our mental health. The debates about retail's psychological effects have been going on almost since the establishment of advertising as a field. As architects, we should not ignore issues like this. We may be in the best of all positions to help elevate these discussions to levels of appropriate complexity.

2003

Notes

1. The current bible for retail anthropology is Paco Underhill's *Why We Buy: The Science of Shopping* (New York: Simon & Schuster, 1999); Underhill had been writing articles and appearing on National Public Radio many years prior to publishing this book. The most useful sociology books were written by William H. Whyte, particularly *The Social Life of Small Urban Places and City: Rediscovering the Center*, for their insight into how people interact in public places. More recently, Ray Oldenburg's *The Great Good Place: Cafés, Coffee Shops, Community Centers, Beauty Parlors, General Stores, Bars, Hangouts, and How They Get You through the Day* (New York: Paragon House, 1989) is an excellent examination of social interaction in public/retail settings. There is so much to draw from in psychology, but two of the more profound books are Abraham Maslow's *Toward a Psychology of Being* (Princeton, N.J.: Van Nostrand, 1962) and *Motivation and Personality* (New York: Harper, 1964), with its theory of a hierarchy of human needs. Ernest Dichter wrote several useful books, including *Handbook of Consumer Motivation: The Psychology of World Objects* (New York: McGraw-Hill, 1964), *The Strategy of Desire* (New York: Doubleday, 1960), and *Motivating Human Behavior* (New York: McGraw-Hill, 1971). Another resource to understand what motivates people is the books related to the Enneagram, including Helen Palmer's *The Enneagram: Understanding Yourself and the*

Others in Your Life (San Francisco: Harper & Row, 1988). In demography, the two most influential sources are the monthly magazine *American Demographics* and *The Clustered World: How We Live, What We Buy, and What It All Means about Who We Are,* by Michael J. Weiss (Boston: Little, Brown, 2000).

2. See, for instance, Theodore Levitt's *The Marketing Imagination* and, in it, his 1960 essay "Marketing Myopia"; Michael Porter's writings on competition and strategy, which started appearing in the early 1970s; Al Ries and Jack Trout's landmark *Positioning: The Battle for Your Mind* (New York: McGraw-Hill, 1986), which again began with work in the early 1970s; David Ogilvy's *Confessions of an Advertising Man* (New York: Atheneum, 1963) and his *Ogilvy on Advertising* (New York: Vintage Books, 1987); and Philip Kotler's books on marketing management, which started appearing in 1974.

3. From my conversation with a store manager.

4. Vance Packard, *The Hidden Persuaders* (New York: D. McKay Company, 1957).

5. In Linda Obrec, "Marketing, Motives and Dr. Freud," *Detroiter Magazine,* December 1999, http://www.moline-consulting.com/Reinventando/Pagines/conceptoDeLasMotivaciones.htm.

6. In 2002, "a subsidiary of Omnicom Group, Inc. of New York, one of the world's largest advertising and corporate communications companies," bought Design Forum, a "nationally known retail design firm." "Leading Ad Company Buys Design Forum," *Dayton Daily News,* February 12, 2002.

6

Rocking for the Clampdown: Creativity, Corporations, and the Crazy Curvilinear Cacophony of the Experience Music Project

Thomas Frank

The Experience Music Project in Seattle is a cavernous, "interactive" museum of popular music history. Constructed at great expense by Microsoft billionaire Paul Allen and housed in a billowing, bubbling, neon-colored structure designed by Frank Gehry, it is an artifact of "New Economy" ebullience as surely as are the motivational posters sold by Successories or the mountains of Enron souvenirs that can be found on eBay. The EMP's position immediately next door to the beloved Space Needle strikes many Seattlites as blasphemous, and the building's blob shape has evoked comparisons in the local papers with dead bodies, with melted quantities of this and that, with feces.[1]

Unfortunately, it was nighttime when I caught my own first glimpse of the EMP in October 2001, so I could not make out the spectacular curving walls that have so challenged the descriptive powers of the op-ed writers of the Pacific Northwest. I was on my way to the museum's Turntable restaurant, where the aesthetic experience was entirely different from what I expected. From the vantage point of my dinner table, I thought the celebrated structure looked like a damaged Costco or an oddly shaped Quonset hut. Ducts and beams and chicken wire were plainly visible, and the light fixtures were simply suspended from pipes overhead. Brutal utilitarianism: check. Then there were the bentwood chairs, and the restaurant booths each shaped like a box open on one

Frank Gehry, exterior of Experience Music Project with Space Needle, Seattle, Washington, 2000. Photograph copyright Lara Swimmer/Esto.

side and with another box above, only with the top box placed insouciantly off kilter, so the geometry was conspicuously "broken." Postmodern playfulness: check. Then there were the waitstaff, bustling about in Mohawks and piercings and tattoos and shirts like the gas station attendants' uniforms that my friends and I found so ironic in the 1980s. Alternative: check.

It was not until the next morning that I gazed upon the famous exterior of the EMP in all its blue, red, and gold swoopiness. Its placement at the base of the Space Needle struck me not as scandalous but as the inevitable second half of a classic phallic pairing: a lumpy postmodern Perisphere to the Space Needle's ultramodern Trylon. I walked around the structure and took due note of the oddly shaped windows, the absence of right angles, the sculpted uniqueness of every wall and every surface, the glass-and-pipe structure snaking along the top, and the neat-o blown-curtain effect next to the tunnel that the monorail passes through. It was indeed very cool.

At first the contrast between the smooth, streamlined external sheathing of the EMP and its jagged, all-exposed interior struck me as evidence of a colossal contradiction. One face of the building was all illusion and undulating curves and crowd-pleasing ornament; the other was the stripped-down exposure style that Gehry was famous for

Frank Gehry, Experience Music Project, interior view of complex geometries from stairs, Seattle, Washington, 2000. Photograph copyright Lara Swimmer/Esto.

back in the seventies. Monumental on the outside; provisional on the inside: perhaps the plans for two or maybe three buildings had been confused.

But the design makes sense when considered in the light of the EMP's larger mission. As the visitor quickly learns, the museum's purpose is not merely to display music artifacts or even to explain the development of certain musical styles but (in the words of the official press kit) to "celebrate and explore creativity and innovation as expressed through American popular music and exemplified by rock 'n' roll." The artifacts and the history are simply a means to an end, the end being the greater glory of "creativity" and "innovation."

And the same is true of the building's architecture. While its different styles may not cohere in any aesthetic way, each of them is strenuously, ostentatiously "innovative."

As is Frank Gehry himself, at least in the corporate world's image of him. There is today no greater champion of "innovation" than management gurus, and for them Gehry has become a living, breathing symbol of creativity. It makes little difference for this school of thought *how* Gehry's work diverges from the boxlike corporate style of the postwar years, just *that* it does, that it incorporates all sorts of wacky building materials and irregular angles. And in those wacky materials and those irregular angles the gurus find an affirmation of the principles of their beloved New Economy: entrepreneurship instead of top-down bureaucracy, frenetic change instead of stability, the chaos of free markets instead of regulation, labor "flexibility" instead of job security. In Gehry's high-profile box-breaking they see a heroic reflection of their own much-celebrated outside-the-box thinking.

A typical bit of guru Gehry-worship can be found in the just published treatise on corporate creativity *New Ideas about New Ideas.*[2] In this new age, it insists, "innovation is the only way to a better time," and innovation in turn can only come from people and organizations that are "hot, hip, and happening." Since nowadays "the artist is more valued than the manager," business leaders must become more like artists, must look to artists as models in both their personal and professional lives. Naturally Frank Gehry is the artist who stands above all others in such a hierarchy, thanks especially to his work for the art-appreciating insurance magnate Peter Lewis and for the brand-building Guggenheim chain of museums. The book repeatedly finds in Gehry's sinuous shapes and his computer-assisted creative process a pattern for the way business must be conducted in the new era we supposedly inhabit.

Strangely, the book then goes on to name Enron as one of the corporations that has most fully internalized these lessons. The great architect and the great corporate thief are linked elsewhere as well: not only does a Gehry building appear in one of the transgression-celebrating TV commercials that Enron used to run, but Enron actually sponsored the recent Guggenheim exhibition dedicated to his work. In a foreword to the exhibition's official catalogue, Jeff Skilling—a former Enron CEO and a man so immersed in "New Economy" theory that he was still talking proudly about Enron's "creativity" when testifying to one of the congressional committees investigating him—wrote that in the architect's "innovative" ways Enron saw a reflection of itself: "This is the search Enron embarks on every day, by questioning the conventional to change business paradigms and create new markets that will shape the New Economy. It is the shared sense of challenge that we admire most in Frank Gehry, and we hope that this exhibition will bring you as much inspiration as it has brought us."[3]

To read Gehry's works as an architectural analog of Enron's swirling, circling, crooked, complex, and remarkably "innovative" accounting practices would be taking Skilling's interpretation a little too far. But Skilling's words do give a sense of the degree to which Gehry became the preeminent architect of the exuberant New Economy moment, his trademark computer-assisted curves representing the giddy religion of entrepreneurial "creativity" in the same way that the Beaux Arts works of McKim, Mead & White radiated imperial grandeur, in the same way that the office blocks of Skidmore, Owings & Merrill symbolized efficiency. In buildings like the EMP—and the Nationale-Nederlanden Bank building in Prague and the Weatherhead School of Management in Cleveland—the chaos-loving corporate theory of the nineties found its consummate physical expression. This is why Gehry-like curves and box-breaking protuberances now grace the offices of the hippest ad agencies and the hottest tech firms.

The specific "New Economy" figure behind the Experience Music Project is Microsoft cofounder Paul Allen. The third wealthiest man in the world, an enormous fan of rock music, and a person who identifies strongly with the Pacific Northwest, Allen spent an estimated $240 million building the EMP.[4] Some have characterized Allen as an unremarkable person swept to undeserved riches by the greatest economic wave of all time. And perhaps the EMP, this rock 'n' roll shrine, is what any regular guy would want to do if he had that kind of money to throw around. But Allen is not just a fortunate bystander or a fan with far too much money. As he likes to explain in interviews, he is a man of ideas, a visionary of what he calls a "wired world" in which creative entrepreneurs generate endless new products and everyone is hooked up to an ethereal electronic web. And the EMP, Allen's "gift to Seattle" (as *Fortune* magazine once described it), is supposed to be as fully realized an expression of this vision as is the portfolio of companies that Allen has chosen to buy.

Not surprisingly, Allen's fingerprints are everywhere in the museum. He personally commissioned Gehry to design the building and then intervened in the process a number of times.[5] The original idea for the place was as a showcase for Allen's large collection of Jimi Hendrix memorabilia, an artist on whom Allen remains fixated with a peculiar singularity. And, naturally, the museum is chock full of ultra-high-tech equipment like the stuff that is produced by the companies Allen owns. Visitors lug wireless computer devices around with them to hear the exhibits explained, a rock concert simulator allows patrons to play along with some anthemic favorites, and—paying plinking, tinkling homage to the Allen vision—there is a two-story-high moving sculpture in which computerized steel fingers strum guitars, basses, and banjos.

The EMP also affirms Allen's New Economy vision in a grander, historical sense. It was a commonplace of the corporate faith of the nineties that the New Economy had its roots in the sixties counterculture, that the ferment of Silicon Valley was in some direct way descended from the ferment of the Haight-Ashbury thirty years before. After all, both hippies and hackers valued freedom and experimentation over rules and order, both liked to get high, and neither fancied the more formal business attire of olden days. Plus, think of the former members of the Grateful Dead who now vented their libertarian thunder in *Wired,* of all the wiggy lifestyles that were believed to signify cyber-creativity, and of the hundreds of TV commercials that coupled telecom services or software "solutions" with Beatles lyrics or Hendrix guitar solos. Even *Time* magazine was moved to declare, in a headline from the ecstatic year 1995, that "We Owe It All to the Hippies: . . . The Real Legacy of the Sixties Generation Is the Computer Revolution." And what management theorist of the nineties could really call his latest book complete until he had rounded off his screeching treatise on the change-change-change-it-all New Economy with a tip of the hat to "alternative" culture?[6] The obvious function of this imagined lineage is to grab legitimacy for the business behemoths of the New Economy era, to cast the increasingly powerful corporate world as a never-ending Woodstock, where everyone is free to express themselves however they want—whether by writing software all night long or even wearing jeans to the office.

This is the narrative that is subtly advanced by the EMP. The development of rock music, the visitor learns, is a lesson in entrepreneurship, risk taking, the liberating power of technology, and above all, creativity.

But before we get to that, consider the first of several colossal ironies about the EMP: the rise of the corporation to its present position of near omnipotence is the direct historical product of the conservative revolution in American politics, which since 1968 has been bringing us lower taxes, weaker government, less regulation, steadily diminishing antitrust enforcement, and a cult of digital entrepreneurship that reached its apogee in the late nineties, just as the EMP was being built. However, that conservative revolution did not take place because Americans love corporations or because they wanted to elevate people like Paul Allen above all historical standards of plutocracy: it came from a massive public revulsion with the "permissiveness" and "bad values" and therapeutic excesses of the sixties counterculture, a revulsion that has been periodically recharged in ferocious culture wars against the "liberal elite" and their subversive anti-family ways. But when the time comes for the man who has benefited from this vast political change more than nearly anyone else to bestow upon the world a great personal statement, he builds a monument to the desecration of family values, its richest and most lavish wing being a shrine to Jimi Hendrix, the greatest countercultural figure of them all.

Watching the crowd of uncool middle Americans shuffle silently through the EMP's hypercool exhibits on hip-hop and skatepunk, I wondered how long this contradiction could continue without somehow collapsing in on itself. The EMP is supposed to be a gift to the people, but I couldn't help but see it as a cackling ingrate in swooping steel and glass. Carnegie's libraries offered uplift; Allen seems almost to taunt his square visitors: *Hey, loser! Where are your culture wars now?*

When I first heard that a new rock 'n' roll museum was being built in Seattle, I thought immediately of the Rock and Roll Hall of Fame in Cleveland, which I visited a few years after it opened in 1995. Another pop music museum designed by another trophy architect—in this case I. M. Pei—its objectives are far simpler than those of the EMP. Organized by Jann Wenner of *Rolling Stone,* Ahmet Ertegun of Atlantic Records, and a handful of other showbiz brass, the RnRHoF is an industry museum, a monument to the institutionalization of a very specific style of rock music. It affirms the tastes and decisions of the music industry's bosses and offers endless lessons in the quality and authenticity of the music industry's products. As such it is not so much about rock as it is about rock stars and their belongings. Like the "classic rock" radio format, where favorite songs of the sixties and seventies are endlessly ranked and replayed, the RnRHoF is dedicated to defining rock orthodoxy: rebel musicians are actually voted in by "rock experts" as though it were the Académie française, and the building itself is shaped like a pyramid, recalling Pei's work on the Louvre and signifying the central principle of hierarchy. With a handful of exceptions, the Hall of Fame's criteria are unapologetically commercial: those who sold millions of records are in, as are those who "influenced" such feats; those who didn't sell so well, those who didn't contribute to the development of the industry overseen by Wenner and Ertegun, are out. The relationship between commerce and counterculture is simple and direct: rebellion is a rock-solid pillar of consumer culture, a perfectly ordinary part of the industrial order.

There is no getting around the fact that corporate rock sucks, however. John Strausbaugh, editor of the *New York Press,* gets the "Hall of Lame" right in *Rock 'Til You Drop,* his recent book on the sad phenomenon of geezer rock: "The Hall of Fame operates according to the tastes and diktats of powerful industry figures and 'experts,'" he writes,

> but rock and roll is, at its best, a grassroots, out-of-the-garage, populist music. . . . Rock and roll is *not* just any other American pastime, equivalent to a sport, though many players and promoters of '70s-style stadium rock have tried hard to make it that; anyone who appreciates rock and roll must want to resist the athletic idioms inevitably employed by a rock "hall of fame," the implied notions that Rock Hall inductees are somehow rock's "champions," who were quantifiably better at the sport of rock than other rockers because they "scored" more "hits," or some such nonsense.[7]

The EMP is very different. For all you sneering hardcore kids ready to dismiss Paul Allen's museum for being fake and corporate and not alienated enough, I've got some bad news. The billionaire has got you beat by a mile.

Although posters of the Beatles and the Stones are on sale in the EMP gift shop, there are no exhibits dedicated to either of those bands. The museum's straight narrative section, in fact, goes out of its way to slight the contributions of Elvis Presley and covers the 1960s with exhibits concerning Hendrix , Bob Dylan, Janis Joplin, and Eric Clapton. That's it. The next stage is punk rock, and after that comes an elaborate exhibit on the indie-rock eighties. No Led Zeppelin. No Eagles. No Lynyrd Skynyrd. No ZZ Top. No Jackson Browne. No Bon Jovi, no Van Halen, no Madonna, no Michael Jackson, no Styx, no Foreigner, no Journey, no REO. No Crosby Stills and Nash, no Emerson Lake and Palmer—but quite a bit on the punk trio Sleater-Kinney.

Admittedly, the EMP's history suffers from all sorts of blind spots and gaping holes, but on the subjects it chooses to address it is infinitely more intelligent, more detailed, more sensitive to nuance, and more properly museum-like than the RnRHoF. The amount of information that is available is massive, overwhelming. Everything is explained;

every exhibit has interviews and subhistories to elucidate every angle. I even happened across one in which indie-rock figures from Los Angeles, Minneapolis, and Washington, DC, were all interviewed on the subject of whether it was a good idea to sign with a major label. At the Rock and Roll Hall of Fame, of course, major labels are the culmination of human progress. The suggestion that maybe you shouldn't sign with one when you had the opportunity just wouldn't come up.

In other words, the story that Allen has paid $240 million to blare out to all the world is not the rock orthodoxy burnished and defended for so many years by *Rolling Stone* magazine but the adversarial narrative that regards the music industry, *Rolling Stone,* and most of Jann Wenner's heroes as villains, as bloated manufacturers of pointless, phony youth culture, manipulating bands and broadcasters and audiences and cramming this year's crap down the throats of the public. This is a narrative that regards the corporate rock period of the seventies not as a golden age but as a dead period, that gives nary a damn for Billy Joel's many gold records but that cares deeply about each punk subgenre, all the independent labels, the skateboarders, the college radio stations, the photocopied flyers for the all-ages shows, the gritty bars where the hardcore bands played in the eighties, all the "scenes" in various cities—DC, Austin, Athens, Chicago, Minneapolis, and, of course, Seattle. The RnRHoF is notorious for downplaying punk and indie rock, but here at the EMP it is a huge part of the story. Check out the picture of Darby Crash and his skateboard. The Sub Pop 200. The exhibit on "K" records. The copy of Big Black's 1986 album *Atomizer.*[8]

While the Rock and Roll Hall of Fame is about consuming, the EMP is about making, about rock as a grassroots phenomenon, a movement of do-it-yourselfers. It is an "interactive" museum, as visitors hear again and again, a place where patrons get to play with instruments, to pretend to be in a rock band, and even to enjoy what the press kit calls a "ride-like attraction" in which their chairs buck and jump in time to the music of a James Brown video they are watching. None of those old, top-down master narratives pertain within these swirling, swooping walls.

"Interactivity," though, is fast becoming something of an ideological museum piece itself. A few years ago it was common to hear the most grandiose sort of democratic claims made for "interactivity": through its agent the Internet, "interactivity" was opening up the world to us, was leveling the hierarchies, was frightening the high and mighty. In the aftermath of the "New Economy" fiasco, however, most of us view such claims with a little more suspicion. Today we know enough about Allen's Microsoft to understand that temp agencies do not empower workers, that the reign of "interactivity" permitted monopolies with unprecedented power, that popular participation in stock markets allowed a concentration of wealth that we had not seen since the 1920s. In this sense "interactivity" was an ideological smokescreen, a democratic, do-it-yourself myth that concealed the fantastic growth of autocratic corporate power.

Similarly, the EMP uses punk rock and Seattle's moment of "alternative" glory as a sort of primer on the home truths of the New Economy nineties. It uses rock 'n' roll not to boost the music industry (as does the RnRHoF) but to advance the rebel-corporate views of its founder. A while ago I asked a friend who knows as much as anyone on earth about the history of the Seattle rock scene what he thought Allen was up to with the EMP. Here was his reply:

1. Make a monument (actually, one of many monuments) to himself;
2. Permanently re-image Seattle as a postindustrial town run by and for persons such as himself;
3. Develop and demonstrate hi-tech display gadgetry that can be used in museums, airports, convention halls, stadia, etc.;
4. Get EMP itself to become self-supporting through admissions, merch sales, and corporate donations, providing a pseudo-libertarian model for running a big arts institution without government support (though it sits on land essentially donated by the city).

To this list we need add only one additional item: dress up the ugly business of high-tech capitalism in the Mohawks and studs and winsome Hello Kitty backpacks of alternative youth culture.

To emphasize again: the EMP presents itself as a shrine to "creativity and innovation." The awesome forces that creativity is capable of unleashing are celebrated throughout the complex. What distinguished the "Swinging London" scene of the midsixties? "Experimentation was everywhere." What was Jimi Hendrix's personal studio really like? It was "a place to experiment." What were the college radio stations and independent labels of the eighties up to? They were "dedicated to supporting rock experimentalism." And while you may have thought that punk rock was an angry, corrosive, scoffing protest from working-class kids on the losing end of the new capitalism, what it really was "about" was "empowering and involving youth in creating their own independent culture—a world where you do-it-yourself or it doesn't get done," a description that effectively strips punk rock of content and essentially equates it with Microsoft products as described by Microsoft advertising: "empowerment," independence, getting stuff done. Creativity thus becomes entrepreneurship, the constant opening up of new markets and new avenues of distribution.

We also learn that creativity is an almost magic quality, something that—like the burdens borne by CEOs—is not always understood by the nongifted. Teaching this lesson is the object of the museum's funk-oriented "ride-like attraction." An introductory video that visitors sit through while waiting to board the ride informs them that "the funk is a powerful thing," that "not everyone has the funk." Then the audience is treated to a little homily of artistic inspiration, rendered in stark racial terms: a big-name funk band, equipped with all the lights and stage antics of a Rolling Stones reunion tour, is shown playing in Japan. For viewers acquainted with the business literature of the late nineties, this strikes an immediate chord: in the New Economy days, "Japan" was standard shorthand for the people who didn't get it, who didn't understand the funky democracy of the Internet and the funky online entrepreneurship of the new era. Japan, in other words, represented that part of America that New Economy libertarians found most detestable: tight-assed government regulation and deathly square labor unions, not the zesty free-for-all of markets that they knew to be the way of the future. And sure enough, two Japanese teenagers show up to watch the band and are instructed by a mysterious black American guide in the secrets of "the Funk." "Do you understand what it means to be an artist? The risk every artist takes to make a statement?" the guide asks the lads. No, clearly they do not understand. To learn, they "must jump into the Funk." And that is where the ride comes in. I and the other middle-aged white tourists absorbing this lesson are ushered into a theater where an elaborately filmed funk video plays and our seats do the dancing for us.

Of course, creative inspiration can get so intense that sometimes the call transcends music. The EMP suggests that the highest creative act available to the rock musician is the destruction of his or her guitar.

Smashed guitars, evidence of this otherworldly passion, are all over the place. There is one from Kurt Cobain, one from the Presidents of the USA, and two in the Jimi Hendrix section alone, including the one that Hendrix famously set on fire at the Monterey pop festival in 1967. Frank Gehry's design for the building is said to have been inspired by an arrangement of smashed guitar parts. Allen himself christened the EMP by smashing a glass guitar. And on the cover of the CD that Allen's band released in 1999, a baby in diaper and headband mimics Hendrix's great creative moment, setting fire to a toy guitar with a can of lighter fluid.

At first this destroyed-guitar theme seems merely peculiar, a quirky way for Allen and the EMP to declare their touchingly earnest faith in the awesome power of art. But that's not it at all. The obvious source for this connection between creativity and destruction is not Romanticism; it is the same New Economy literature that worships Frank Gehry and tells us the Japanese don't have a chance. The gurus' preferred phrase is "creative destruction," a term they borrowed from an economist of the forties and applied to the glorious whirl of Silicon Valley in the nineties. What we needed to do, they said, was start smashing things: corporate structures, job security, favorite brands, labor unions, regulations, old ways of doing and thinking about every single little thing. Remember? Only when we had destroyed it all would creativity be properly unleashed to do its thing and make us all rich. "Destruction is cool!" foamed Tom Peters in 1997. "There can be no expertise in innovation unless there is also expertise in demolishing the ensconced," intoned Kevin Kelly in 1998. To which Paul Allen has added, Just do what the rock stars do.

The second great historical story that the EMP tells is a sort of triumphant Pacific Northwest regionalism, focusing especially on the development of the famous Seattle grunge scene of the early nineties when "Seattle became world famous as a music center." All events in the "Northwest Passage" exhibit either lead up to this moment of glory or slope downhill in its aftermath, a version of rock history so unapologetically whiggish that it puts Jann Wenner in the shade. For example, more than once does the museum justify the attention it pays to the esoteric world of indie rock by explaining that this is the stuff that preceded the great grunge explosion. Like all such histories, it also traces the greatness back to ancient times: "people in the Pacific Northwest have been coming together to create music and share it in a communal 'scene,'" runs one bit of exhibit text, ever since "the first Native Americans gather[ed] to dance on these shores."

Given Allen's significant control of Seattle's cultural apparatus—he owns everything from sports teams to the Clear Blue Sky film production company to KCMU, the former radio station of the University of Washington (it was renamed KEXP after his acquisition)—it was more than a little predictable that any rock museum built by him would celebrate the Seattle "scene" as the ne plus ultra of authentic cultural production. Even so, I found certain elements of the exhibit quite compelling, like the detailed exhibit on the many different bands who recorded "Louie, Louie," the rock anthem that is so beloved in the Pacific Northwest.

The discussion of "scenes," though, is consistently carried on in the telltale language of New Economy thought. "Scenes," in this telling, seem to be places where kids get together and start up feisty, soulful companies that then square off against tired, corrupt old-line companies. Thus, the Sub Pop record company, which released LPs by almost all of the bands that would later be identified with grunge, is described as "a visionary label" with a "brazen corporate self-image." And grunge itself? Why, it was "An Idealistic Insurgency," an effort to force "An Industry Power Shift." The earnest kids from Seattle tried their best, they sold all sorts of CDs, "but, alas," as one bit of text puts it, "grunge couldn't force the industry to change its corporate power structure." The clear implication here is that grunge was somehow a grassroots demand for the new style corporation—a historical interpretation that certain management writers have actually made in all seriousness—but that the arrogant big record companies refused, and that is why grunge died.

What actually happened, as the critic Mike O'Flaherty has shown, was that the Seattle scene was absorbed by an industry that was very much aware of its sagging credibility and deeply in need of an authenticity transfusion.[9] It pushed what it called "alternative" rock with every sinew in its corporate being, making that characteristic Kurt Cobain growl immediately as pervasive as the debased pop of the Bon Jovi era. And then, when the inherent contradiction of all that angst on all those Top 40 radio stations became apparent—a contradiction, incidentally, that is repeated a thousandfold by this $200-million shrine to low-budget music—the music industry simply spat the thing out like a cherry pit. That is what happened to indie rock.

But the EMP drowns the dirty particulars of corporate cultural production in a wash of simple caricatures. Whether they are the corpulent big-label executives of Los Angeles or government authorities, the other side is irredeemably stupid and hostile, and that's it. Visitors to the EMP read a boneheaded denunciation of jazz that appeared in a Seattle newspaper in 1921; hear a story about the FBI's effort to stamp out "Louie, Louie"; watch a filmstrip about how LA cops beat up LA punks back in the day.

It was while watching this last that the whole thing came apart for me. As it happens, I visited the EMP with the highly creative Mark Hosler of the band Negativland, which in 1991 put out a hilarious send-up of a U2 song that used lots of sampling—and which got them promptly sued by Island, U2's record label; then by SST, their own (independent) record label; and then threatened with legal action by Casey Kasem, the host of "American Top 40," who is heard cursing and shouting angrily on the record. Although it generated plenty of press at the time, there is no Negativland exhibit at the EMP, possibly because there is no obvious way to present the episode with a clear entrepreneurial winner on one side or the other. Only Negativland, a bunch of outspoken leftists, came out looking good. And neither Allen nor anyone else with a big stake in Microsoft is about to challenge copyright itself.

Anyhow, Mark and I watched a film on the LA punk scene in which Greg Ginn of Black Flag, the owner of SST, appears and expands on the perfidy of the LA police. "That's the guy who sued me!" Mark shouted. Later he and I took to the stage of the EMP's mock auditorium to pretend to play the song "Wild Thing," for which the rights have no doubt been secured well in advance. Mark wanted to test the limits of the EMP's interactivity by giving our band the punk rock name "Paul Allen Is a Poop-Head" but was told by a series of irritated museum employees—in nose rings and dyed hair—that this was neither funny nor acceptable.[10] We were "Positivland" instead, after *The Power of Positive Thinking,* the book that Casey Kasem mailed to Negativland to cheer them up.

My day at the EMP ended with a visit to the "Sound Lab," where museum goers get to do a little hands-on music making and mixing. Naturally, Mark and I headed straight for the "sampling" booth, where we were told to follow the creative trail blazed by De La Soul, a band that, ironically, had once been sued by the same law firm that later sued Negativland. Mark shared his feelings about the EMP with the microphone, and we played the words back as a funk tune, a snappy pop song, and a soothing choral number.

The EMP is filled with warnings about selling out and letting the music industry own the products of your creativity. But the EMP itself may have the grandest designs of all on our creativity: shamelessly cloaking itself in the garb of a great cultural moment, it proceeds to use the democratic, do-it-yourself promise of underground music to teach us something that is in truth deeply undemocratic and disempowering. Punk rock is really entrepreneurship, it informs us. It is really a bunch of new companies challenging a bunch of old companies; its war against the major labels is simply an inspiring preamble to the cyber-revolutionaries' own war on big media. And although there are no doubt dozens of libertarian punk rockers who agree with such an interpretation, it cannot help but do terrible violence to punk's intense class consciousness, to its well-known suspicion of business and industry, to its adamant rejection of the free market orthodoxies of Margaret Thatcher and Ronald Reagan. (On the other hand, the museum's narrative does render in heroic relief such enterprises as the Seattle-based start-up Groovetech.com, a combination online radio station and record merchant.)

The limits of this narrative become painfully clear in the single bit of text that I could find in which the EMP actually addresses the subject of social class. The fact that this happens only once is itself a curious oversight given the museum's regionalism, as the Pacific Northwest was once a place known for its intense class consciousness—its Wobblies, its lumberjacks, the Seattle general strike of 1919. To this day Washington remains a heavily unionized state. But the "creativity" narrative puts the class context in an entirely different light. "Rock 'n' roll," a bit of explanatory text maintains, "is the musical and cultural expression of the Great American Melting Pot theory. You take something from just about every ethnic, working-class culture in America in the first half of the Twentieth Century, mix it up, spread it by every form of mass communication available, and then watch it as it climbs up the socioeconomic ladder." Being working class, in other words, is a condition cured by rock 'n' roll, the great opportunity maker. You don't reduce inequality, you escape it.

Consider also the jaw-dropping disproportion of the thing: Allen has spent more than $240 million on a "music project" to catalog and dissect and research in all its intricate genealogical detail a marginal subculture whose leaders, only a few years ago, were shopping in thrift stores and living in vans. Even at its apogee in the early nineties, all of the assets of the indie rock world combined probably would not have amounted to much more than one-twentieth of that sum. Even more questionable is the attention given to still extant bands and very recent movements, such as the Riot Grrrl phenomenon. Not only is such an effort obviously prone to mistakes and to pranks, but it dramatically contradicts the spirit of the thing. Clearly it changes a "scene"—a "scene" that is still going on, still producing things— when its low-budget, do-it-yourself authenticity is celebrated to the skies by a mega-million-dollar museum that is obviously determined to define who's legitimate and who isn't. This is a form of observation that nukes the observed.

These days things are not nearly so exuberant in the curving halls of the New Economy. The great gurus are keeping a low profile, the CEOs are taking the fifth, and the high-flying stock pickers are trying to explain losses of 60, 70, 80 percent. The cult of creativity that recently claimed so many followers has receded for the moment, no doubt embarrassed to discover the unpleasant synonyms—"deceptive," "manipulative," "criminal"—that now stand alongside such twenty-four-karat words as "innovative." At the same time, attendance at the Experience Music Project, it was reported in January 2002, fell by 35 percent, which in turn caused the layoffs of 24 percent of the museum's staff. Perhaps that is due to the drop-off in tourism since 9/11. But perhaps it is also due to the inherent strangeness of the thing now that the bubble has burst and reality has reasserted itself. A billionaire's love song to alienated youth, the EMP will continue to remind us of a bizarre chapter in our national intellectual life: the corporate rapture, a time when every sound on earth seemed to echo back the wisdom of free markets.

2003

Notes

1. See, for instance, Steve Duin, "Paul Allen: New Colossus or Barney Rubble?" *Portland Oregonian*, March 26, 2000.
2. Shira P. White with G. Patton Wright, *New Ideas about New Ideas:*

Insights on Creativity from the World's Leading Innovators (Cambridge, MA: Perseus Press, 2002). The book's blurb: "*New Ideas about New Ideas* introduces us to a dynamic, eclectic collection of creators, whose far-out and far-reaching experiments are changing the world. Drawing from interviews with dozens of mavericks such as contemporary artist Jeff Koons, technology oracle Nathan Myrhvold, celebrated physicist Brian Greene, and biotech visionary Henri Termeer, Shira White explores the exhilarating process of generating new ideas and bringing them successfully to fruition. Blending important concepts from the worlds of management, the arts, science, and technology, Shira White reveals profound insights into what makes today's most creative people and organizations tick. You'll meet Corning chairman, Roger Ackerman, who led a series of extraordinary corporate transformations; genius architect Frank Gehry, who shocked the world with his earth-shattering Guggenheim Museum in Bilbao; pioneering Progressive Insurance chairman, Peter Lewis, who records his flashes of brilliance while swimming; Satjiv Chahil, who made Palm a household name; and many other innovators. *New Ideas about New Ideas* is bound to change the way you look at your life, your work, and your world."

3. J. Fiona Ragheb, ed., *Frank Gehry Architect* (New York: Guggenheim Museum Publications and Harry N. Abrams, 2001).

4. David Kirkpatrick, Paul Allen, and Bill Savoy, "Why We're Betting Billions on TV," *Fortune Magazine*, May 15, 2000, http://www.fortune.com/indexw.jhtml?channel=artcol.jhtml&doc_id=00001247.

5. Apparently to the annoyance of the architects. "[T]ensions over interactivity and its goals surfaced during the EMP's long gestation," writes Lawrence Osborne in *Metropolis*. "One designer who worked on the project early on and who wishes to remain anonymous, says that the original aspiration to create an idealistic temple to American popular culture became lost in the fortress mentality of powerful corporativism: a paradox that Paul Allen carries within himself: 'Their thinking became closed, proprietary, competitive, and totally geared towards money and commodification. It was not what I signed up for.'" "Kiss the Sky," *Metropolis*, May 2000, 109.

6. One example, from many: super guru Gary Hamel, who insists in his book *Leading the Revolution* (Cambridge, MA: Harvard Business School Press, 2000) that "business concept innovation" is the inescapable way of the future, exhorts his readers to become "revolutionaries," "activists," "heretics," to hang out at "the hippest club in your city," to imagine themselves shocking the corporate hierarchy the way a kid in "green hair and an eyebrow ring" shocks his parents (59, 117, 188, 134, 136, 200).

7. John Strausbaugh, *Rock 'Til You Drop: The Decline from Rebellion to Nostalgia* (London; New York: Verso, 2001), 186. See also Strausbaugh's discussion of the Hall of Fame's obsession with rock stars' possessions, 183.

8. As you have probably guessed, the EMP is also remarkable for the way

in which it institutionalizes professional rock criticism. Although it might be utterly foreign to most of the museum's visitors, the EMP's chosen narrative—everything from its reverence for the Sleater-Kinney to its disdain for the classic rock seventies—is quite familiar stuff for anyone who has read the works of the nation's most prestigious rock critics. Just as the RnRHoF enshrines the views of the music industry, the EMP enshrines critical expertise. The museum employs a number of A-list rock critics as curators and in April 2002 hosted an academic-style "pop music studies" conference, "Crafting Sounds, Creating Meaning: Making Popular Music in the U.S." The abstracts of the papers presented make for fascinating reading simply by themselves: http://www.emplive.com/visit/education/pop_music_panels.asp?pD=0412.

9. Mike O'Flaherty, "Rockerdämmerung," *The Baffler 12,* 1999.

10. According to the Web site "Eat the State," http://www.eatthestate.org/05-16/PaulAllensSecret.htm, EMP volunteers are required to sign an agreement that they will not discuss "EMP, Paul Allen, or Mr. Allen's family, friends, business associates or business or personal interests" with "members of the media" and even that they will not "disparage" Allen or the EMP in any way.

7

Rockbottom:
Villa by OMA
Wouter Vanstiphout

"... une condition trés ... ahum, ahum, ahum ... intéressante," the voice booms in a big brick warehouse, between broken bodies swinging suspended from the rafters and immense steel spiders loitering around children's bedrooms. Above, in the galleries surrounding the big space, are tight phalanxes of youth concentrating on television sets, themselves being watched over by severely dressed art femmes. This is not the new Metallica video. Rem Koolhaas is giving a lecture at the opening of the Office for Metropolitan Architecture (OMA) exhibition "Living," in the Centre d'Architecture Arc en Rêve in the Musée d'Art Contemporain de Bordeaux, which is currently running a show by Louise Bourgeois, the French artist responsible for some of the most unsettling images in contemporary art. A thousand people have shown up. A hundred are sitting in the actual lecture hall; the rest have to make do with televised Koolhaas. The exhibition features four villas and an apartment project, all of which have been built and are lived in. The main feature, the reason that the place is teeming with foreign critics and curators and French politicians, is to be found somewhere else.

For that you have to leave the building, take a left, follow the heavy traffic to the north over the quay, where the cars, trucks, gas stations, and discotheques are incoherently juxtaposed against the elegant Louis XV sandstone riverfront. Then take the bridge over the river, follow it for a couple of kilometers, drive inland through a sprawl of identical suburban houses and industrial buildings; take a winding road up the leafy hill until you reach a private dirt road that brings you farther up. To your left lies a pasture with a ruin of an eighteenth-century tempietto, behind it an elegant neoclassical mansion, and in front of you, on the top of the hill, a reddish brown box punctured with holes. On top of the box lies an I-beam that sticks out on one side and is connected to the hill by a spidery steel rod, making the box look like a balloon tethered so it won't drift away on the wind. As you come closer, the box appears to hover over a cut stone perimeter wall. The dirt road is carved into the hill and burrows its way underneath the wall into the courtyard.

The gradual unveiling of OMA's long-awaited "Maison Bordeaux" reaches its climax here. As a model, the house was published a couple of years ago. The model can be seen in the exhibition, but now the house can be visited with the architect and the client. Later, at a "right moment," OMA—displaying the fastidiousness about images that seems to be an unavoidable part of architectural dinosaurdom—will allow the world to see a small selection of glamourpics, bringing even more

Rem Koolhaas, interior of Maison à Bordeaux, Bordeaux, France, 1998. Photograph copyright Cassandra Wilkins.

visitors up the dirt road. But now, this afternoon, there is the extraordinary opportunity to see for the first time what the real house looks like and simultaneously be there.

But if the whole sequence of events resonates with house, living, being there, and other similar feelings of closeness to architecture, then why, at the vernissage, does Koolhaas lecture about China's nonspecific, nonarchitectural, faraway, depersonalized, nonauthentic, quantity-based, not-there posturban conditions? Why does he sardonically state that in China architects produce ten times as much, ten times as fast and do it ten times as cheaply as their European counterparts and therefore can be said to be a thousand times as good, and say this at the opening of an exhibition of projects that have taken an ungodly amount of design time, for small fees, only to make something desperately unique, utterly authentic, personal, and seriously Architectural?

Does this have anything to do with the post-*S,M,L,XL* Remchasm between practice and theory? With the fact that right after finishing work on the big book, Koolhaas took a teaching position at Harvard on the condition of not having to teach design, so he could undertake huge fact-finding expeditions into the Pearl River Delta, Shopping, and Africa? After the meshing of seeing, writing, designing, and building in his baroque gem of a book, he now imposes a stark distance between writing about things and making things. The concentration on making hyperspecific buildings and the obsessive curiosity about the world are now presented as two separate, sometimes conflicting fields of action. This is a dramatic departure from the formula that has made this architect a star: by letting the descriptions and readings of Manhattan, Singapore, or Lille meld with urbanistic designs or even architectural objects, a kind of architectural and theoretical parallel universe was created: Remworld, paranoid-critically coherent, accessible, imitable, exciting.

Well, kids, Remworld has shut its gates! You are invited back to reality, back to life. The stuff happening in Shenzhen, Sudan, or a shopping mall is there, for real, completely unaffected by our or anyone's interpretation. At the same time, the projects that are presented are not the models of a semifictional urbanoid future but are here, now, in your face and under your arse. The discrepancy between the two destroys any hope for a coherent philosophical, methodological, or even narrative system out there that might connect them. We have hit rock bottom. Now it's for real.

Living

The house has been built for a wealthy publisher, his family, their guests, and some cars. The publisher was paralyzed from the waist down after a car crash—a rubber-burning, steel-twisting, bone-splintering, marrow-leaking, nerve-splitting car crash. The design is, among other things, a monumental accommodation to this fact. In no way does the architecture attempt to glaze over the minutiae of everyday life with architectural elegance and solemnity, as so often happens in villa design. What actually happened is that Rem Koolhaas has feverishly imagined architectural potential in this particular family's life. He saw the limp lower body of the husband—supported by a whole arsenal of trusses, carts, belts—as architecture. He extrapolated this in a single huge, heavy-duty contraption that provides the man with a way of moving through the house. Subsequently this contraption was made into the house's organizational core ("A machine was its heart":[1] going up, going down, going up, down, up . . .). In counterpoint to this hydraulic simplicity, the beautiful and lithe wife moves through the house at will, negotiating between the armpits and crotches of the house and its dematerialized, entropic, smooth, modernistic planes. Koolhaas also saw architectural potential in his constructionally counterintuitive decision to place the chromium tube on which the box-house lies off center, so that a huge beam had to be placed and then anchored in the ground with a big rock, to stop the house from toppling over.

Visitors cannot look at the house as an architectural model that can be separated from its specific usage. The usual gaze of historians, critics, or architects won't do. In fact, you are investigating the most intimate and personal details of this specific family's life; the gaze is that of the babysitter wandering through the rooms, opening the drawers, and looking in the medicine chest. At the same time, because in a way the family's life has become architecture, the villa becomes strangely inclusive: a design equivalent of MTV's soap vérité, The Real World. Lastly, the specific demands and wishes of this family are dealt with not so much on an architectural level as on a planning and engineering level, emphasizing infrastructure, technical facilities, zoning, and routing. The family's life has been treated as an urban program that makes the house into a "New Town" and makes a visit to it an unexpectedly civic experience. The mode of description that this house seems to ask for is therefore a combination of abject speculation by a voyeur about the private lives of his desired objects and an urbanistic scenario in which different propositions are linked together by a hypothetical sequence or route.

A day in the life: Early in the morning; after he has been placed in his wheelchair, the glass wall slides open, and he moves into the kitchen, passes the monolithic concrete stove, and slips behind his desk set in a lofty skylit space. Behind him, a sea-green resin bookcase goes up three stories. A knobless door opens into a dark cavern containing the bottles of claret. On the desk lies an industrial remote-control device, a telephone, a newspaper, and a workbook for learning Mandarin. He pushes the remote control, and the room moves up; he slides past the bookcase. It is possible to stop at any point and take out a book—for instance, *S,M,L,XL*.

After a couple of meters, the room locks into the floor of a stunningly glassy glass house, the metallic floor flush with the hill. The man looks down into the parking space in between the perimeter wall; he looks the other way over Bordeaux and the river; he looks around and sees some furniture and also a huge chromium cylinder and a thin rod, both connected to the big box floating above the living room. He drives off the platform toward the view, goes into the garden where the path burrows into the ground, and looks inside a flower. He drives back in, maneuvers himself behind his desk, and makes his room go farther up. He locks into the third floor; through the bookshelves he

Rem Koolhaas, exterior of Maison à Bordeaux, Bordeaux, France, 1999. Photograph copyright Cassandra Wilkins.

sees the terrace. Next to him Gilbert & George's "Lifehead" looks apotheotically skyward.

He moves away again and passes a number of physiotherapy contraptions, crosses the terrace, and goes into the master bedroom. His wife is still sleeping. He quietly passes the bathtub, goes past the white resin washing slab: a face floating by in the mirror. Back in his study, he sits a while behind his desk. One porthole in the wall is precisely positioned to give him a view of the horizon; another is aimed downward to give him a view of the hill. A therapist arrives and gives him a workout. His wife helps him get into a different wheelchair for his shower. The water disappears in the cracks between the floorboards. From where he sits with water running over him, he looks in the split separating the adult half of the top house from the children's part and sees himself reflected twice in the glass. Then his wife dries him off and helps him into the hospital bed for a nap.

She takes a bath, gets dressed, and crosses the metal grate bridge between the two parts of the top house into the children's quarters. This half of the box is divided by diagonally placed walls that strangely remind you of the folded door/walls around Louise Bourgeois's children's bedrooms at the exhibition and, like those, seem saturated with memories and nightmares. She wakes some kids, springs open some of the glass plates covering the portholes, and takes a medievally tight and dark spiral staircase—hidden in the chromium tube—down two stories into the TV room. She follows the curve of the wall into the kitchen, makes herself some coffee and a croissant, takes it back in front of the TV, and watches the Breakfast Show. She then gets up and enters a strange uterus-like staircase that takes her to the living room.

Now she is surrounded only by huge glass walls; she slides away some of them and walks over to the end of the metallic floor, where she looks out over smog-covered Bordeaux. In the middle of the living room is a big square hole with a hydraulic steel shaft supporting the platform, which is now locked into the top house of the house. Through the hole she peers into the kitchen. She walks back behind the bookcase where her desk stands. She settles down to look at her e-mail; the wires of her PowerMac sway in the wind. After a while, when the children are all ready, she rushes up the concrete stairs glued to the bookcase and wakes her husband. He and the children will leave for the afternoon; she will receive the architect and a group of guests who are extremely impatient to inspect every nook and cranny of her home.

The house demonstrates the Paranoid Critical Method as a radical way of deploying the heat-oppressed brain in architecture. Explained in (pop)Kantian terms, the P.C.M. can be understood as a psychologically charged relationship between the world as it exists by itself, regardless of whether there is a human observer to interact with it—noumena—and the world as it appears to us humans—phenomena. Koolhaas's Paranoid Critical glare makes the noumena acquire such an obsessive intensity in the way they manifest themselves in the brain of the beholder—as phenomena—that they can be turned into architectural facts and returned to the world as new noumena loaded with fear, love, disgust, angst, ennui, lust. The reality of this family has become hyperreal in architecture. The product is what we might call a concentration of phenomenally noumenal phenomena, or noumenally phenomenal noumena.

The Attack of the Haptic Experimentalists

However, in January 1998, Dutch architects Ben van Berkel and Caroline Bos published a critical article about Rem Koolhaas's work in the magazine *Archis,* in which they set off Rem's "semantic-analytical approach" against the "Haptic Experimental line taken by Zaera Polo and kindred architects" (which they also follow, as do Greg Lynn, Jeffrey Kipnis, Sanford Kwinter, et al.). "Now that the more experimental approach is rapidly on the rise—witness, for instance, Gehry's Guggenheim Museum in Bilbao—it is feasible that Koolhaas's influence may decline in the coming years."[2] There are two extremely peculiar ideas in this little quote: first, to hoist poor old Frank up on the table and make him King of the Haptic Experimentalists; second, to prophesy a backlash against Koolhaas by starting it. This is why they stress the feasibility of Koolhaas's decline instead of its possibility.

It is no wonder that as soon as Koolhaas broke up the quasi-theoretical limbo in which even his built work seemed to linger, and his work could no longer be seen as diagrams, models, or icons of his or anyone else's writing, the rift between him and his Haptic Experimentalist counterparts opened wide. The economy of avant-garde architecture in American universities requires a certain homogeneity of writing, design technique, and architectural form. But Koolhaas seems to have abandoned this. His jumping off the bandwagon is a gesture that can be taken as an omen for some radical changes in the critical landscape of architecture and thought, changes that maybe not everyone can adapt to. A decline in the influence of Koolhaas would at this point perhaps be comforting to the Haptic Experimentalists. (But whether trying to effectuate this decline is the best way to secure their future remains doubtful.)

The harsh criticism by Van Berkel and Bos is partly fallout from the ANYhow conference in Rotterdam in the summer of 1997, where Haptic Experimentalism tried to manifest itself as the new avant-garde with a non-manifest manifesto, hesitatingly read by Sanford Kwinter. Koolhaas then launched repeated attacks against the introverted formalism of this group. "The line" taken by Haptic Experimentalism is that there can be real life, or real intelligence, or real excitement in the morphogenesis or emergence of form brought about by experimental design techniques, computers, datascapes, mapping, and so on. H.E.s even go so far as to say that architects' thinking lies entirely in the semiautonomous design process: in the model, the computer screen, or the crayon on paper.

To people who are not theosophically or otherwise mystically inclined to believe that there is intelligence in the semiautonomous production of blobs and lines inside computers, it is hard to find any thinking at all in the architecture of Haptic Experimentalism. As becomes apparent from Van Berkel and Bos's article, the line holds that Koolhaas applies techniques like folding and collage so rigidly that they remain "verbal constructs" and only "acquire three-dimensional identity at a much later date." The only way to define the "future importance" of Koolhaas's oeuvre is to subject it to a formalist research, to divorce the "formal manipulations" from the "verbal constructs." The hypothesis seems to be that when OMA buildings are not surrounded by Koolhaas rhetoric, they will appear not to be so interesting after all.

Picking apart Van Berkel and Bos's novel approach to Koolhaas helps us to focus on the tragic and morally uplifting beauties of the villa in Bordeaux. First, Van Berkel and Bos's argument that Koolhaas uses collage and folding in a rigid way means that they understand content and visuality as architectural form, as is indeed apparent from their own work. They see even the Paranoid Critical Method as a historical architectural motif having to do with form. As classic art historians, they present a set of stylistic attributes, call these formal manipulations, and designate these as the critical center of the oeuvre. In other words, Van Berkel and Bos place the identity of the work in the way the design techniques become directly visible, much as Bernard

Berenson located the identity of the master of a fifteenth-century panel in the brushstroke. This was an important part of Berenson's theatrical performance as the connoisseur and the basis on which he could sell the panel to American art collectors. Maybe a similar way of thinking about architecture also makes sense to the Haptic Experimentalists, as a basis on which to sell their particular avant-gardist styles to state universities.

Second, saying that Koolhaas's architecture is semantic implies that he uses signs to denote . . . well, that which is denoted. How can we understand this? Is the moving platform a sign for the crippled man? Is the superpositioning of the houses a sign of collage, of super-positioning things? Is the house a sign of living? Is the whole design a three-dimensional diagram of a linguistic formula denoting the life of the family? I think not. Just because the Paranoid Critical Method is expressed in language and is also implemented in architecture does not mean that the architecture is a piece of language. And because the house presents itself and is presented in terms of program does not mean that the house denotes the program.

What makes the house is that it is a bit of world in your face; the world is neither denoted, as Van Berkel and Bos imply, nor broken down into data and fed into an interiorized process of formal ma-nipulations, as is the case in designs by Van Berkel and Bos and their fellow H.E.s. The world has become architecture, not by abstraction but by inclusion or rather intrusion. To put it in the terms of the great theoretician of form and believer in the real, Gilles Deleuze (a philoso-pher often quoted by H.E.s), the fact that the guy is crippled, or rather that a car crashed, is the "difference that is given," the "intensity" that "actualizes the virtual form" that is the house: a form that did not, even as a possibility, exist before.

Gary Bates, architect at OMA, confessed that when he saw the house for the first time, he was "fucking scared, because it raises the stakes even higher." It does. It raises the stakes of how far OMA dares to let the real in. After this house the world cannot as easily be cen-sored before being let into architecture: radical-chic caricatures of life can no longer be so easily translated into formally inventive master-pieces. It is one thing to present innovative architectural ideas against the backdrop of Far Eastern statistics and an ever-expanding, ever-progressing generic metropolis. Engaging the small, the personal, the painful, and the sad, and doing it beautifully, is another thing. Here is an architecture that has more to do with steel spiders, broken bodies, and children's bedrooms than with its own vocabulary of form or with a parallel universe of imminent hypermodernization. During ANYhow, Koolhaas asked Greg Lynn: "Are you a mystic?" We eagerly ask Koolhaas: "Are you a humanist?"

1998

Notes

1. Office for Metropolitan Architecture/Rem Koolhaas, *Maison à Bordeaux, OMA* (Rotterdam, 1997).

2. Ben van Berkel and Caroline Bos, "Formal Manipulations: OMA's Educatorium," *Archis* 1, 1998: 8–15.

8

Inside the Blue Whale:
A Day at the Bluewater Mall

Rick Poynor

Before I went to Bluewater, if someone had asked me what I thought about the idea of this gigantic new shopping mall in the suburbs of London, my answer would have spoken volumes to an impartial observer—a sociologist, say, or the kind of market researcher that a mall developer might commission—about my background, expectations, and prejudices. I hesitate to add "class" to the list only because in Britain the received wisdom, in the past ten or fifteen years, especially among the political classes, is that we are becoming a "classless" society. True to type, without having seen Bluewater, I would have condemned the ultimate—and quite probably the last—British shopping mall as a cynical, ecologically unsound cathedral of commerce, a vampire development sucking the life out of ailing high streets in nearby towns, a non-place as characterless and sterile as the contemporary airports it so much resembles.

Shopping malls, as the British social critic Paul Barker has observed, bring out the English vice of snobbery on both left and right. "The attacks on the shamelessly populist designs of the shopping malls follow in the footsteps of the earlier onslaughts on 1920s suburban semis or 1930s super-cinemas, on 1950s TV aerials or 1980s satellite dishes. The motto often seems to be: Find out what those people are doing, and tell them to stop it."[1] Ironically, though, what the middle classes

Eric Kuhne, interior of Bluewater Mall, Greenhithe, England, 1999. Photograph copyright David Spero.

find objectionable today as a manifestation of vulgar working-class culture, they have a tendency to treat as "heritage" a generation later. "I await, with confidence," concludes Barker, "the first conservation-listed shopping mall."[2]

The criticisms of Bluewater after its opening in March 1999 followed this all too predictable path. *Blueprint* magazine's editor, for one, could not hide his disdain: "Many millions of people will visit Bluewater this year. They will laugh and shop and eat and say they like it. They will be greeted as 'guests' in the 'welcome halls' and 'groom' themselves in the loos and eat in the 'break out areas.' It would be patronizing to tell them to stop it."[3] But patronize Bluewater's millions he does (not that many will have subscriptions to *Blueprint*). "What kind of people are so scared of rain or cold, so lazy that they can't walk up hills, so frightened of alleyways or a darkening sky?" he demands to know. "Catering for them only reinforces their paranoia and threatens to destroy the rituals of real town centre shopping."[4] Another of *Blueprint*'s writers, finding a shop interior she can bring herself to recommend among the hundreds of retail units, scoffs at the shoppers' unseemly behavior. "You almost feel that the whole shop could be slid out of its hole and driven away if the company ever changed its mind about Bluewater. Which given that the clientele have taken to standing and clapping every time the drawbridge is opened or closed, might not be a bad idea."[5]

The tone of these dismissals made me more intrigued by Bluewater than I might otherwise have been. I found myself wanting to test my own preconceptions with a visit. These writers sound determined not to be impressed, as a matter of principle, and the intellectual position behind their criticisms—other than snobbery—is unclear. What are these cherishable rituals of town center shopping? What is so wrong with clapping if you enjoy a special effect? The writer takes Bluewater's shop designs to task for not being adventurous enough but seems to regard the fashion shop she does admire as being almost too good for its nonmetropolitan clientele, who fail to respond to its design values with the right degree of sophistication and restraint.

Bluewater is eighteen miles east of central London, a mile or so from the River Thames, in a place called Greenhithe in the county of Kent. Among Bluewater visitors, I belong to an underclass. The mall, a destination conceived for drivers, like all such developments, has 13,000 parking spaces, but I do not drive a car (or want one). I take the forty-five-minute train journey from London to a tiny station, where the railway signs now say "Greenhithe for Bluewater." It is Friday morning, and a regular shuttle bus transports me and a few other carless shoppers—mainly young women—to the nearby mall.

The despoiler of high streets lies, half-hidden, in a reclaimed quarry surrounded by chalk cliffs. From the outside, Bluewater is a jumble of gray forms, sprawling low and flat in the landscape, largely undistinguished except for the angled ventilation cones on its roof, shaped like Kent's oasthouses, which give it the look of an aerial tracking station. I wander along the side, cross the boardwalk over a lake (one of seven), and enter the Wintergarden, a glass and steel canopy inspired, we are told, by the Palm House at Kew and said to be the largest greenhouse built in Britain in the twentieth century. Pathways meander between the trees and restaurant seating areas. It is like being in the atrium of a tropical hotel.

The two-story building's plan is triangular. Each side is a distinct zone with its own theme, design style, atmosphere, and type of store. The Wintergarden leads to the Rose Gallery (typical high street shops), and depending on which way you turn, this eventually takes you to the Guildhall (glitzy fashion labels, designer homewares) or the longer, gently curved Thames Walk (toys, sports, games, street fashion). These sectors also have their own recreational spaces and eating areas, which spring from the sides of the triangle. A shop-lined passage, modeled on London's Burlington Arcade, connects the Guildhall to the Village, and the Thames Walk is served by the livelier, clublike Water Circus. At each corner of the triangle there is a domed entrance, also themed, to one of Bluewater's three "anchor" stores—John Lewis, Marks & Spencer, and House of Fraser—the dependable retailers of middle-class Britain.

Early research by Lend Lease, the Australian owners of Bluewater, showed that nine million people live within an hour's drive of the site, and they are among Britain's wealthiest consumers, with an annual expenditure 32 percent higher than the national average. Four out of five fall into the A, B, or C socioeconomic groups used by marketers. More than 72 percent of the homes in this region are owner-occupied and have access to a car.[6] Further research, in the form of a questionnaire, led to the division of this catchment into seven "clusters," accounting for almost five million people. These categories were given names to reflect their lifestyle characteristics. Highest in spending power, and therefore of greatest interest to Bluewater's developers, were the "County Classics" (wealthy, usually married, having wide interests and concerned with home, entertaining, family, and quality), the "Club Executives" (successful, married, quality-conscious, liking to be in control and prepared to pay extra for convenience), and the "Young Fashionables" (single, in their early twenties, image-conscious, brand-oriented, active).

All three groups preferred to do "serious" shopping in central London. To convince them to choose Bluewater, the mall would have to match the experience, quality, and range of retailing in London's smartest shopping areas. The mall visionaries pursued this goal with a vengeance, attracting seventy-two stores from Covent Garden and fifty-eight from King's Road, many of them agreeing to venture out of London for the first time. Camper, the Spanish shoe company, had just a handful of stores in some of the capital's snootiest addresses (Brompton Road, Knightsbridge, and Bond Street). Others prepared to dip their toes into Bluewater included Calvin Klein, Diesel, French Connection, and Muji, the "no brand" minimalist home store. Three hundred and twenty shops now occupy 1.6 million square feet of retailing space.

Bluewater promised these status-conscious outfits that they would rub shoulders with similar establishments. It painted a seductive picture of a "retail experience" that went far beyond the usual perceptions of even the most successful British malls. Special attention would be paid to "sensory factors" such as surfaces, materials, and air quality. Creating a sense of welcome was vital. The need for safety, expressed by many potential customers during research, would be a matter of overriding concern realized in every design detail. The restrooms, often hidden away down long corridors, would be situated in the welcome halls, which customers would enter directly from the adjacent garages, and these halls would be like hotel lobbies, with a concierge on hand to help guests, and coffee bars, where people could pause to get their bearings.

The architect charged with developing these concepts is an American, Eric Kuhne.[7] Even critics who abhor Bluewater gush with enthusiasm at his "charm," "erudition," "educated manner," and skills as a speaker. Kuhne visualizes the project in the grandest of terms. "We've really designed a city rather than a retail destination," he says.[8]

This is fighting talk to those who take the view that the last word to use to describe a place like Bluewater is "civic." But if one of the things we value in real outdoor city spaces is the possibility for people to meet, converse, interact, pass the time, and enjoy a shared public life, then Bluewater offers pleasures and satisfactions that the mall's more hostile commentators have been reluctant to concede. For a commercial space, it is prodigiously supplied with nonpaying seats not connected to cafés, many of them comfortable leather armchairs. Soon after I arrive, I pass three women in their sixties, one wearing a knee bandage, talking about a friend's swollen ankles. It is unlikely they belong to Bluewater's favored socioeconomic clusters, and they do not seem to have bought much. This is not a place you pass through, however, on the way to somewhere else, so they probably came on the bus just to be here with their friends and relax. I am struck by how few people carry shopping bags (though the day is still young). Bluewater has forty or more places to eat, from upmarket French bistros to sushi-on-a-conveyor-belt bars, but at lunchtime, I notice a young woman settle down in a leather chair, place her lunch box on a side table, and unwrap a homemade sandwich.

Of course, all this attention to sensory factors and quality of experience is not motivated by altruism. Bluewater is a machine for making money, and these are the lubricants that increase its efficiency. The parkland outside is there to help visitors "recharge their batteries," explains the celebratory Bluewater book (a sign in itself of the mall's ambition). The unstated hope is clearly that rather than flopping into the car and driving home, the recharged shopper will return to the aisles with a spring in her stride and credit cards at the ready. The book half expects our disapproval and makes a brief attempt to brush it off: "To say, as some inevitably would, that there was something underhand about this would be tantamount to writing off every piece of design-for-profit that had ever been built or produced. The environments were intended to seduce, and in that way, Bluewater was no different from a designer dress or a piece of exclusive furniture."[9] This is a painfully thin defense of consumerism, but it has a point. If the aim is to sell good design, and this is acceptable in luxury design shops in London, aimed at the trendy, loft-dwelling classes, why is it unacceptable ("sinister" according to *Blueprint*) for such things to be made available to a much wider public outside London, in the suburbs?

Class may not be a word that British politicians like to use these days—it suggests inequality and unresolved struggle—but it remains a significant factor in British society. Ordinary people clearly think so. A Mori survey in 1991 showed that nearly four in five believe that the country "has too many barriers based on social class." A Gallup poll in 1995 indicated that 85 percent subscribe to the existence of an underclass.[10] Britain's classless society is a myth, argues a widely acclaimed indictment of our social structure by political journalists Andrew Adonis and Stephen Pollard. We might not like to admit it, but we are all experts at reading the signals and giveaways of class. "Accents, houses, cars, schools, sports, food, fashion, drink, smoking, supermarkets, soap operas, holiday destinations, even training shoes: virtually everything in life is graded with subtle or unsubtle class tags attached," write Adonis and Pollard.[11] But these signals are becoming increasingly scrambled. You can buy cappuccinos as well as baked beans on toast in a motorway service station. Social mobility abounds, and almost everyone is better off today, even if the gap between the top and the bottom of the income scale grows apace. As the authors explain, "most of the 'working class'—meaning manual workers—leads what even a generation ago would have been considered a middle-class consumer lifestyle."[12]

Bluewater shows just how far this process has come. It offers an experience that many of its visitors would not or could not easily have had before it arrived in their midst. It recognizes the consumer behavior of different social classes within its many zones, but this multiplicity, the sense of things to discover, encourages people to wander and explore, and they do. Drinking coffee in the Mise en Place café in the Village—its dark wood cabinet windows clearly conceived with the "County Classics" in mind—I watch a couple arrive with their daughter, no older than four. The man has cropped hair, tattooed biceps, a beer belly, combat trousers, and boots. His keys hang from a belt loop. They have come to take the little girl to a film. She is bored, restless, and has to be encouraged into an armchair. "You want to go to the pictures?" the man says gently. "Well, sit down." He pushes the chair toward the table. He is not entirely at ease, and you can tell this is not the kind of place he would usually frequent. "There are rules and regulations," he tells the little girl.

Yet Bluewater aspires to be something greater than a social melting pot in which all visitors are notionally equal in the sight of the pound. In Kuhne's imagination, it is a "city," and this is not only a matter of size and services, although a poster really does boast that Bluewater is "Twice the size of Bath city centre"—that is, equal to one of our most beautiful, historic cities, and even *bigger*. In its attempt to relate itself to its environs, in its faux monuments and its elaborate literary program, Bluewater strives to endow itself with nothing less than the trappings of civic meaning, as though these ordinarily gradual accretions to a city's fabric, the statues and inscriptions, could be willed into existence and achieve gravitas overnight.

Do visitors pay any attention to these decorations and texts? I saw no evidence that they do. The only person pausing to study the sculptures or read the epigrams was me. In the upper mall of the Thames Walk, verses in four-foot-high capitals about Old Father Thames rolling along to the mighty sea form a frieze that runs the length of the mall. It is impossible to read at a glance, and few will walk the entire length for this purpose. In the Rose Gallery, lines waxing lyrical on creamy, dreamy roses, fresh as morning's birth, are plonked on an I-beam under a monotonous trellis of artificial roses—easily the most impoverished of Bluewater's displays. At every turn archways and entablatures are adorned with words by Rudyard Kipling, Robert Graves, Laurie Lee, and other Kent writers. The Roman lettering is obviously intended to be monumental, but it is invariably overpowered by the loud typography and jangling colors of the shop fronts, an unwitting reminder of the triumph, everywhere, of commercial communication as the dominant form of public address. The hollowness of the literary sentiments in this context is underlined by the shoddiness of the appliqué lettering, which awkwardly straddles the cracks between the stone blocks.

In the Guildhall, Britain's 106 guilds—loriners, shipwrights, clerks, and tallow chandlers, and others—are represented by sculptures in niches. Again, the quality of craft and manufacture of these lumpish figures is poor. They look like relief carvings, but there are empty spaces behind them so you can see they are just flimsy moldings. Far from dignifying visual art as a source of higher meaning, these devices reduce it to the level of visual Muzak, shallow and irrelevant. Any of the stores will themselves offer finer examples of design and workmanship.

This attempt to dress up the commercial machinery of Bluewater in a layer of culture and "class" is patrician and patronizing. It tries to pretend the mall is something other than it is, and then having taken the cultural path, it loses its nerve, rather than commissioning real artists to create unexpected and challenging experiences. Culture is treated as a Linus blanket, to coddle the visitor, and the arts are demoted to empty decor. I doubt consumers are taken in by these cultural pretensions, though. They almost certainly do not care. While the art might contribute vaguely to the ambience, the primary features of the interior design—the use of timber, limestone and leather, the ornamental balustrades, the lamps like harbor buoys, the "sails" hanging in the Thames Walk—carry more weight.

I came to Bluewater expecting to despise it. What I discovered is that while you can hate the idea of Bluewater, it is harder to hate the experience itself. It was easy to spend time there. Five hours passed quickly. The place was kind to the senses, unexpectedly relaxing, and I could have stayed longer. I did not feel oppressed. If I lived closer, I would probably go again. Maybe this is its cleverness: it lulls and anaesthetizes.

As Bluewater's critics inadvertently revealed, once the routine arguments about the economic and environmental damage caused by this development have been stated, a convincing case against the place is hard to make—a case that would be persuasive to someone clutching bags of shopping after an enjoyable afternoon at the mall. What would you say? How would you convince the shopper that he is wrong? For the cultural critic Bryan Appleyard, struggling with this dilemma, Bluewater encapsulates a moment of transition to what he calls a "new order." Appleyard rehearses the arguments of the traditionally educated person—someone like himself—with a conception of human progress, values, and ethics derived from Greco-Christian-Renaissance-Enlightenment culture. "I could easily imagine the newspaper columns I could write deriding this place," he notes. "Its architecture, although fine and lovely, is depraved. The staff are robots. It pollutes. It glorifies the empty pleasures of consumption. Its superfluity is trivial. . . . Its artificiality suppresses seriousness and depth."[13] And yet, he concludes, he could not write such a column because his response is much less simple than that.

Right now, as I discovered, the arguments for and against Bluewater are *both* true. But when we complete the transition to the new order of abundance it represents, suggests Appleyard, the case against it will cease to make sense. As he notes, most of our values were formed by historical conditions of scarcity. The new conditions of plenty make those values not just redundant but also incomprehensible to most. For many visitors, Bluewater is as luxurious as it gets, spectacular local evidence that prosperity is growing and twenty-first-century living is good. So, once again, as the shopper loads his bounty into the car—what exactly is our objection? Appleyard puts it this way: "If 2,500 years of intellectual and physical struggle were not meant to achieve this, what were they meant to achieve?"[14]

Eric Kuhne, interior of Bluewater Mall, Greenhithe, England, 1999. Photograph copyright David Spero.

But again, this is too simple. The struggle is not over. Bluewater, despite its police station, multiplex cinema, and bus garage, is not a town. It is a controlled, private space. The lower-class Ds and Es—to use the marketing lingo—can turn up if they like, but with little cash in their pockets and few aspirations to upward mobility, they are not part of the plan, and they had better not step out of line. No drunks and crazy people here, thank you. No beggars. No street musicians. No gangs. No protesters. No disorderliness of any kind. No wonder we fall for Bluewater. It is secure, tidy, a Pleasantville vision of Utopia—or rather, it is a vision of Utopia for some. To let yourself be lulled by it is to collude with the politicians' rhetoric of classlessness, to forget the ideal of social justice, to pretend that the old class tensions between the haves and the have-nots no longer exist in Britain, and having blanked them out of the scene, to abandon the neediest people in society to the town centers we no longer care to visit.

It may be that no more malls will be built in Britain. Many of the public say they prefer them, but government policy has changed, and planning permission is being withheld.[15] Perhaps the country will set about regenerating its high streets at last. Many are degraded spaces. Blighted by long-term neglect, ravaged by the car, they offer little to compete with the safe, weather-free, indoor cornucopia of places like Bluewater. But there is minimal evidence to suggest that we have the political determination, the public vision, or the public money to re-invent the civic and to appropriate retail design's understanding of sensory experience for the noncommercial public realm. Our vehicles have helped to corrode our townscape; so doing further damage, we drive somewhere else, where the cars are at least kept at the door. If declining town centers are to reawaken, it will be by embracing the new order and becoming surrogate malls.

2000

Notes

1. Paul Barker, "Malls Are Wonderful," *Independent on Sunday,* October 28, 1998, 9.
2. Ibid., 12.
3. Marcus Field, "Tragedy in the Chalk Pit," *Blueprint* 161, May 1999, 45.
4. Ibid.
5. Fiona Rattray, "Bluewater or Ditch-water?" *Blueprint* 161, May 1999, 47.

6. Research quoted in *Vision to Reality* (London: Lend Lease, 1999), 60.

7. Kuhne was given the title "concept designer." He had never designed a shopping mall before. His practice, Eric Kuhne & Associates, is known for parks and civic spaces. The project architect, supporting and developing the design process, was Benoy.

8. Field, "Tragedy in the Chalk Pit," 45.

9. *Vision to Reality,* 73.

10. Andrew Adonis and Stephen Pollard, *A Class Act: The Myth of Britain's Classless Society* (London: Penguin, 1998), 4.

11. Ibid., 10.

12. Ibid.

13. Bryan Appleyard, "The Age of Plenty," *Prospect* 41, May 1999, 46.

14. Ibid.

15. Dan Roberts, "Shoppers Prefer Out-of-Town Sites," *Daily Telegraph,* November 19, 1998 (source: *Electronic Telegraph*). Research by the British Council of Shopping Centres found that four of the top five shopping destinations were away from traditional shopping areas. Preferred sites were the Metro Centre, Gateshead; Lakeside, Essex; Meadowhall, Sheffield; and Merry Hill, West Midlands.

9

We Dig Graves—All Sizes

Daniel Naegele

In small-town Missouri, for amusement, on Sundays, we shop. So several weeks ago, needing nothing but having heard rumors of the arrival of a new line from the East, I aimed my RX-7 at the town's only Target. There, to my delight, household accoutrements from the onetime "Cubist kitchen king" abound. Tastefully packaged in blue and white cartons, all items are titled and come complete with a square photo of the designer, his signature, his bar code, and the following credo: "The Michael Graves product line is an inspired balance of form and function. At once it is sensible and sublime, practical and whimsical, utilitarian and aesthetically pleasing. Michael Graves creates useful objects, which not only carry their own weight, but simultaneously lift our spirits." How very hardworking and communal, I thought; and in need of spirit-lifting of the sensibly sublime sort, I began to buy. Wine glasses, measuring cups, tongs, table clock, pizza cutter, scrub brush: all eventually assembled themselves that afternoon on my dining room table.

Not until the next morning, however, did I fully understand the import of "carry their own weight." It was 7 a.m., and as I squinted half awake at my new Michael Graves alarm clock, its hands and their shadows conspired both to conceal the "12" and to complement its face with a Nixon-like nose. At the time, too, its "3" and "9" metamorphosed

Table Clock, 1999. All designs by Michael Graves for Target. All photographs by Vito Alula.

Pizza Cutter, 1999.

Wine Glass, 1998.

Measuring Spoons, 1999.

Scrub Brush, 1999.

Tongs, 1998.

into eyes (their gray rectangular fields suggesting corrective lenses), while the "6" offered itself as a slightly open mouth. Clearly, Table Clock was squinting back at me, and only then did I notice his soft-shoed feet and mittens, cupped to support his ever-so-swollen face. Poor TC, I thought, perhaps he has been stricken by mumps or fallen victim to Marathon Man dentistry.

It was then that the others presented themselves. Morning light transformed Pizza Cutter to a shimmering, albeit big-headed, ballerina. With outstretched arms and a banana biomorphic body, she dons leotards of blue Santoprene—dishwasher safe and stylishly cut to reveal her stainless steel naval.

Scrub Brush, by contrast, appears pleasantly plump yet always in a state of distraction. Wearing an overly round countenance and a baseball cap with upturned beak beneath a hemispherical hood, he would pass for a not-so-distant relative of Southpark's Kyle or Kenny were it not for the cylindrical garden of white bristles sprouting from his face.

The Measuring Spoons are a family of four—papa, mama, baby sister, and big brother. With their hollow hemispherical heads, elongated necks, and oval bodies, they are refugees from a Max Ernst painting. Curious dressers, they go bottomless but sport blue T-shirts with "Graves" embossed on the back.

Like the others, Wine Glass has a distinctly tripartite corpus composed exclusively of discreet geometric shapes. All glass and an essay in circular sections, his huge head sits atop a cylindrical *piloti* trunk, itself supported on feet in the form of a glass circle. He is reserved and aloof and a bit too transparent, and hovers rather distantly above mere utensils.

My favorite, though, is Tongs. Obviously Asian (with a name like that), at first he appears only as silhouette, a two-dimensional paper doll of stainless steel, sensuous in his sleekness, radiant yet irresolute in his reflectivity. When taken in hand, however, he is rotund, a buoyant body that begs to be clicked like castanets. He, too, wears a T-shirt, but of a minimalist sort: nine blue Santoprene balls displaced in square formation across the abdominal zone. One can imagine Tongs as a kind of Futurist gingerbread man cut from a vast sheet of stainless steel, sprinkled sparingly with delectable dots, then neatly folded into a springy doppelgänger, both silhouette and shadow. One can imagine him, too, as a streamlined toy soldier or an Asian Charlie Brown, or even a metallic bowling pin—this latter association being particularly possible in mid-MO, where many an evening's entertainment is found at "the alley" (and where any mention of cuisine art almost surely will provoke commentary to the effect of "Why quiz Art? He never did know nothin."). The most polyvalent of the group, Tongs might also be seen as a surrogate hand with beefy forearm, or looking "inside" of him from above, an illusory mirrored landscape of sinuous lines and evocative forms.

Now it is certainly true that "Missouri Loves Company," so such delightful guests are always welcome.[1] Nevertheless, I suspect a rather spotted pedigree for this task force of gadgets: cartoons and Max Ernst, of course, but also Man Ray's anthropomorphic imagery of now-primitive kitchen accessories, the exquisite "plop-drop" teakettle handles of Josef Hoffmann, Miro's effervescent dancing moons, and perhaps the stretch-neck figures of Picasso's late-1920s portraits. And since in Michael Graves we have a born-again designer, the family tree might be enlarged to include the two Corbus: the young *"machine à habiter"* Le Corbusier, as well as the matured, post-Hiroshima, *"faire une architecture c'est faire une créature"*[2] cosmological Corbu. But nothing in this ancestry seems as puppy playful as its Target protégé. Graves's objects follow us home, amuse us when we least expect it, relieve the tedium of the mundane, and occasionally permit us an aggressive moment. (How I love to grasp the chunky ballerina in hand and push her headfirst into a deep-dish pizza, to twiddle between thumb and forefinger the fragile neck of Wine Glass until he squeals in anguish, to ruthlessly rub Scrub Brush's face in it, or to callously plunge Tongs into a big vat of boiling oil, whistling while I work!)

So Michael Graves—prolific not only in the production of architecture but more importantly in the making of icons that alter one's way of thinking about things—has offered in these objects not the ugly and the ordinary but rather the extraordinary. Useful, inexpensive, available to all, open to suggestion, and imbued with an indomitable optimism, his working toys of wit and whimsy epitomize the age of image in which we live. They transcend class barriers. Their essence resides in their purposeful ambiguity, and it is this artistically calculated quality that permits nonelitist mass production some vague yet palpable sense of authenticity.

Or does it? And are these "presences"—undoubtedly amiable and amusing—really as innocent as they appear? The question is provoked by two remote but resonant concerns. First is the vague resemblance of Graves's anthropomorphic items to those found and framed, not so long ago, by certain Surrealists as well as by Le Corbusier. In this older work, such presences suggested anything but frivolity and entertainment; rather they recorded a somewhat sinister otherworldliness. Does the "fun" nature of these new millennium figures render them innocuous, or should we regard them as even more suspicious because of this guise? Second is the realization that the Target implements, cuddly and cute as they are, are also the result of a carefully constructed theory of architecture, a theory intent on the production, or perhaps more accurately, on the resuscitation of representation. That is to say, the Target toys embody, in a miniature and distilled fashion, Graves's theory for a built environment. Yet unlike his buildings, they are ubiquitous, working their "sublime, practical and whimsical, utilitarian and aesthetically pleasing" selves into the everyday lives of everyday consumers.

A few examples should suffice as elaboration on the first point. During the Second World War, Le Corbusier, exiled in the Pyrenees but still painting daily, decided to "set aside for a while the figure of man" in his work. Instead, he took stones and pieces of wood as his subject for somewhat abstract pictures. Reviewing these abstractions several years later, he came to the surprising conclusion that the "wild rumblings" of this difficult wartime period had "filled the atmosphere with obsessive presences." He was astonished to find that the fragments of nature that he painted then had, as he put it, "led [him] on involuntarily to draw beings who became a species of monster or god." In recounting this episode, he stressed that while making these paintings he had no knowledge whatsoever of "beings" residing in them. Only after some four years did he find the figures, calling them "Ubus." Ubu was "a powerful and ludicrous person created by Alfred Jarry," he later explained, a figure "reincarnated in a thousand places in our present world."[3]

Finding such figures changed Le Corbusier's understanding of painting. He now saw this undertaking—always for him a precisely controlled act of presentation—as an involuntary externalization of a hidden interior, a creative act in which a hidden stratum buried deep in the subconscious was uncovered. Painting might serve to exorcise the portentous spirit of the time or unconsciously to re-present another artist's (Jarry's) earlier creation. Following this revelation, Le Corbusier began to cast his work in cosmological terms, invigorating his architecture with a dimension that spoke not of the Machine Age of the 1920s and early 1930s but of a psychological continuum, a kind of substratum, of mythic ages of past millennia.[4]

Le Corbusier was hardly original in uncovering such presences; rather, he followed the work of certain Surrealists—of the photographers Man Ray, Maurice Tabard, and Brassaï, for instance, who in the interwar years captured on film "reality contorted into signs." Carefully cropped and lit, a man's torso with upraised arms bore uncanny resemblance to the head of a bull, or the shadow from a pilaster base took on the appearance of the silhouette of man's face. Phenomena of this sort were discussed regularly in Surrealist journals by Max Ernst,[5] Georges Limbour, Georges Bataille, Carl Einstein,[6] and others, perhaps most explicitly by Salvador Dalí in his 1931 "COMMUNICATION: Visage paranoïaque."[7] There Dalí recalled how he was "looking for an address in a pile of papers when suddenly I was struck by the reproduction of a face I thought was by Picasso." Subsequently, the face disappeared. What Dalí had seen was a magazine photograph of "natives" sitting in front of a domed hut with hills and clouds in the background. The photograph was intended to be read horizontally, but he had viewed it vertically. His essay included three images: the horizontal photograph, the same image turned vertically, and the vertical image enhanced to convey its likeness to a Picasso portrait. For him, this apparition served as a revelation of the inner psyche of the viewer, and he consulted André Breton, who interpreted the face not as a Picasso portrait but as belonging to the Marquis de Sade.

In Dalí's and Le Corbusier's descriptions as well as in those of their contemporaries, it is suggested that the world is not at all obvious and absolute but rather composed of many layers, some hidden. Special perceptive faculties are necessary to access or "receive" these hidden layers. Artists were considered especially adept at translating such signals into legible signs. And certainly, twentieth-century developments in psychology, physics, and technology reinforced this outlook. Freud postulated a mind distinct from, yet residing within, the body. Einstein declared the physical world not absolute but relative. The invisible medium of electricity, with its capacity to do work at a distance and seemingly without effort, began to replace noisy, muscular, and highly obvious mechanization. X-rays recorded hidden interior structure. Radar and sonar constructed what Le Corbusier later would call "acoustical space." Radios and eventually televisions transformed signals that surround us into audible and visible formations. Time and space coalesced, and with each new decade, new worlds were awakened.

Such radical re-formations, I suspect, did not alter the soap-box-derby, suburban Indiana world of the young Michael Graves; rather, they *were* that world. In America, in the prewar decades, moving pictures, high-speed travel, radio broadcasts, and rapid and remote communication began to distance humans from the material reality that for centuries had been the basis of existence. Ultimately, these and other innovations ushered in an "age of image," a distinctly different brand of "reality" that reached cruising altitude in the 1980s. It was then that Graves—who had begun his career in the late 1960s by dropping the neo-Corbu Hanselmann house into a middle-class Fort Wayne neighborhood of Phony Colonials and French Provincials—wrote "A Case for Figural Architecture." His view of architecture as text and his strategies for resuscitating its representational presence were very much of their time.

Graves opens this carefully considered treatise by postulating two kinds of forms that "exist in any language or any art": standard form and poetic form. He applies this distinction to architecture, noting that the "standard form of building is its common or internal language," and the poetic form of architecture is "responsive to issues external to the building, and incorporates the three-dimensional expression of the myths and rituals of society." From this he concludes that "if one's goal is to build with only utility in mind, then it is enough to be conscious of technical criteria alone. However, once aware of and responsive to the possible cultural influences on building, it is important that society's patterns of ritual be registered in the architecture."

Graves notes that the Modern Movement "based itself largely on technical expression" rejecting the "human and anthropomorphic representation of previous architecture." In so doing, it "undermined the poetic form in favor of nonfigural, abstract geometries." Its promotion of aesthetic abstraction was beneficial in that it "contributed to our interest in purposeful ambiguity, the possibility of double readings within compositions." But, by and large, the Modern Movement's overwhelming interest in technical expression—that is, in its own internal language—resulted in the failure to develop a true external language, a language that "engages culture at large," a language "rooted in a figurative, associational, and anthropomorphic attitude."

Inferred in all this is that the Modern Movement achieved only a "standard form of building" and that a superior architecture will actively cultivate an external language. Graves offers examples of ways in which one might accomplish this. Windows, for instance, should not be walls but instead should meet our expectations by somehow being "coincident with the waist of our body." The "thematic differences between various parts of the whole" should be clearly identified by changes in "material, textural, chromatic, and decorative inferences." Building should involve "association with natural phenomena (for example, the ground is like the floor), and anthropomorphic allusions (for example, a column is like a man)." Graves goes on to suggest that a "larger, external natural text within the building narrative" might be developed, and he observes that the soffit is commonly thought to be celestial and that other elements of the building might "reinforce such a narrative," thus cultivating "the full text or language of architecture." He further suggests a "tripartite division of the wall into base, body, and head," not to imitate man literally but rather to stabilize "the wall relative to the room." Finally, Graves calls for an architecture, like that of Palladio's Villa Rotunda, "comprehensible in its objecthood" and with an interior volume that "can be read similarly." In closing, he insists—here employing the Barcelona Pavilion as example—that the "lack of figural reference" in Modern Movement architecture "contributes to a feeling of alienation in buildings" and that the "cumulative effect of nonfigurative architecture is the dismemberment of our former cultural language of architecture." Unless architecture once again begins to represent "the mythic and cultural aspirations of society," he warns, its cultural continuum is at risk.[8]

In this treatise, Graves never states why Modern Movement architects dismissed representation and the "objecthood" of Palladianism, or, indeed, why they focused so intensely on technique. It is assumed that they embraced both a machine aesthetic as well as a Darwinian notion of progress, and that such persuasions clashed with the representational and figural; certainly there is much to support this view. But given the "material world" into which these Modernists were born, and given the subsequent trend throughout western Europe and America toward a reality comprised more and more of imagery and simulacra, it seems entirely plausible that their motivation was more conservative than progressive. There is, for instance, Paul Klee's 1920s observation that "the object is surely dead. The sensation of the object is of first importance."[9] Could it not be that one reason for shunning the representational, the figural, and Palladian "objecthood" was that such *a*llusion suddenly seemed part and parcel of an unreal world of *i*llusion—of a "sensational" world that was everywhere replacing "reality" and in so doing threatening the very essence of architecture? And could it not be that one reason for underscoring technique and for "dismembering" the "former language of architecture" was a fervent desire—conscious or unconscious—to counteract the threat of representation replacing reality? And wouldn't making the materiality of buildings as obvious and indisputable, as palpable, real, and present as possible serve this cause? Which is to say that rather than working *against* "cultural continuum," Modern Movement architects and their followers might have been working *for* the preservation of reality as they knew it. Insisting on a nonreferential architecture, they sought to resist the apparent frivolity of an illusory world, a world so often associated with the highly suspect entertainment industry.

One could read the movements of Modernists in this way. In the early teens, for instance, Frank Lloyd Wright left the artificiality of suburban Chicago for the farm fields of Spring Green and eventually for the more feudal culture of Japan. He began growing buildings of fieldstone and raw wood, carving them of lava rock and later weaving them of concrete block—techniques that resulted in rooted, inert, and above all "honest" building. In Berlin, in the early 1920s, Mies van der Rohe called for an "organic" architecture of "uncompromising truthfulness." He sought a "renunciation of all formal lies" and housing "clearly dictated by function and material." He illustrated this plea with a tepee, a leaf hut, an Eskimo house of moss and seal fur, an igloo of snow and ice.[10] His villas lost their frontality, shed the pose of Palladian objecthood, to relish in the *Sachlichkeit* of brick and concrete construction. In France, in the mid-1930s, Le Corbusier abandoned the machine-age metaphor and the slick vocabulary of Chareau's Maison de Verre in favor of the vaulted, bermed, and primitive. His tiny Maison de Week-end and Maison aux Mathes were Depression-era preludes to the brutal and starkly natural mode of concrete construction that he discovered in Entreprises Limousin's colossal wind tunnel of Chalais-Meudon, the perfect model for his coarse, elephantine, postwar buildings at Marseilles, La Tourette, and Chandigarh. In America, beginning in the mid-1950s, Louis Kahn insisted on a natural palette, on rooms that reveal how they were made, on an absolute order and a tectonic directness, and on a heaviness that made his buildings seem like immutable blocks—entities older than their sites, older than the light that illuminates them. Each of these overt expressions of "technique" was intended, one might surmise, to root man's existence in material reality, or conversely, to counter the rapidly approaching age of image. Each, I suspect, was construed to reject the fabrication of "an external natural text within the building narrative" in favor of a more immediate, less mediated rapport with nature.[11]

Graves, of course, is not of the age of resistance and reality but of the age of acquiescence and image. He equates architecture with literature and thus with mediation. Architecture is allusion; its component parts, simile. The "ground is *like* a floor." A "column is *like* a man."[12] His view is toward a decidedly non-present "presence"—the sensation of the object—and the buildings that he builds of this sensation seem the very essence of this era.

Unlike in the far more "modern" work of Robert Venturi (whose buildings are wrapped in representation but still flaunt, through their layering, the manner in which they are made), in Graves's buildings there is no "it" to wrap. His is a thoroughly integrated and homogenous manner of re-presenting representation. Graves builds buildings that are *like* representations of buildings; he paints a building into which we can walk. The 1980 Portland Building, for instance, seems so much like a graphic that it effectively calls into question the "real" buildings that surround it. And when Graves designs a commemorative cookie tin that resembles the Portland Building, he represents representation (à la Duchamp's *Boite-en-valise*), distilling his strategy to essential but simple components: a conventional *objet-type,* the canister; a simple cube; the appliqué of stylized color to form a facade. In this souvenir reproduction, Graves underscores the essence of what one senses at Portland: that here stands not a building but the idea of a building "comprehensible in its objecthood."

Graves's later works elaborate and refine strategies and sensations introduced at Portland. All are comprised of simple, fundamental shapes (circles, squares, triangles) that define simple volumes (cylinders, cubes, pyramids). Like forms found in a de Chirico painting, these volumes already exist in our imagination. They are as much diagrams or ideas as they are material entities. Timeless and abstract, they can be employed at the scale of a tea service or a twenty-six-story office tower, found in plan as well as in elevation. Though rotundities and overt volumetric "solids" abound in this architecture, it is the infra-thin layer of color that impresses itself most on the viewer. Graves builds with color; his materials are phenomena. His coloration does not dematerialize the building so much as it etherealizes it. In no way natural or specific to a particular building, Graves's color palette is instead his signature, the inescapable presence of his style. With it, Graves represents Graves.

Unable to eliminate the factor of firmness, Graves cultivates a technique that hides technique. His buildings are like full scale models but intentionally so. To straddle the line between representation and reality, he conceals how and of what his buildings are made, thus effectively elevating representation to an aesthetic plane exclusive of material concerns.

Graves's buildings bear little direct relationship to the natural world, to their specific sites or to cosmological movements. This is not to suggest that his architecture is failed or flawed, rather that he has convincingly created a kind of phenomenal, referential environment, one appropriate to the world of image in which we so often dwell. His best works are those in which function coincides with fantasy, works intended to evoke a theatrical or imaginary world—Disney's Swan and Dolphin Hotels, Cincinnati's Riverbend Music Center, Napa Valley's Clos Pegase Winery, showrooms and boutiques, even libraries and gentrified gymnasiums. Indeed, Graves's architecture makes us aware of how much of contemporary life demands overt representation as setting. His works offer a picture frame or proscenium. They effectively separate fiction from reality but place everyday activities on the *fictive* side of the frame. In an age of image, all the world is a stage, and where Modernists once found meaning in remaking reality, we ourselves find it largely in making appearances.

I have tried to answer by example not only the question, "What happens when architecture becomes representation?" but also and more specifically, "What happens when architecture becomes representation in the age of image?" Modernists uncovered and framed reality as coded. Graves, on the other hand, creates a coded world to complement an already illusory world of synthetic sights and sounds. His Target line—with its anthropomorphic representation, purposeful ambiguity, tripartite division, and parts differentiated by material, color, and texture—goes beyond the mandate of "A Case for Figural Architecture." At Target, one buys not the Portland Building but the commemorative tin. Any semblance of originality, authenticity, or even exclusivity is lost with mass production and coast-to-coast department store distribution. But origin and authenticity are rooted in old-world reality. That Graves allows them to evaporate is not surprising.

In the current age of hyperreality, an architecture that represents representation might be seen to serve as cultural continuum, for it embodies the very essence of the age. But is this the continuum that Graves had hoped to achieve? That we dig Graves goes without saying. But in a time when one employs a telephone receiver to "reach out and touch," or "visits" a "site" by staring at a computer screen, such an activity certainly involves nothing so real as a shovel.

2000

Notes

1. Shortly after finding myself in Missouri, thinking it imperative that tourists be told about this state, I wrote the governor to suggest that the state motto be changed from the decidedly doubtful "Show Me State" to the more congenial and descriptive "Missouri Loves Company." My letter remains unanswered.

2. Le Corbusier, from section "E.4 Caractères" in *Le Poème de L'Angle Droit* (Paris: Editions Verve, 1955), 136. For elaboration on Le Corbusier's cosmological tendencies, see my "*Un Corps à habiter*: The Image of the Body in the *Oeuvre* of Le Corbusier," *Interstices 5* (Auckland: 2000), 8–23; and my "The Image of the Body in the *Oeuvre* of Le Corbusier," an essay in the collection *Le Corbusier and the Architecture of Reinvention* (London: Architectural Association Press, 2003), 13–39.

3. Le Corbusier, *New World of Space* (New York: Reynal and Hitchcock, 1948), 21.

4. *Le Poème de l'Angle Droit,* begun in the 1940s but published in 1955, is the primary written manifestation of this new perspective, Ronchamp and the Brussels Pavilion the primary built manifestations.

5. See, for instance, Max Ernst's "Du danger qui existe pour un gouvernement d'ignorer les enseignements du surréalisme" in *Documents* 34, 1, June 1934, 64–65, in which he finds the face of Lenin hidden in *la propagande communiste camouflée,* and various obscene images hidden in renowned works of art by Leonardo, the Elder Lucas Cranach, and others. See also in *Documents* Ernst's "Beyond Painting" in which he tells of an incident when, alone at an inn on the coast, he "made from the [floor]boards a series of drawings by placing on them, at random, sheets of paper which [he] undertook to rub with black lead." While "gazing attentively at the drawings," he was "surprised by the sudden intensification of [his] visionary capacities and by the hallucinatory succession of contradictory images superimposed, one upon the other." Finally, his "eyes discovered human heads, animals, a battle that ended with a kiss . . . "; Max Ernst, *Beyond Painting and Other Writings by the Artist and His Friends* (New York: Wittenborn, Schultz, 1948), 7.

6. See, for example, in *Documents* 1, 1929: Carl Einstein, "Pablo Picasso,

quelques tableaux de 1928," 35–47; Georges Limbour, "Chronique: Paul Klee," 53–54; Georges Bataille, "Le Langage des fleurs," 160–68.

7. Salvador Dalí, "COMMUNICATION: Visage paranoïaque," *Le surréalisme au service de la révolution* (Paris, 1931 [12.3]), translated in Massimo Cacciari, "Animarum Venator," *The Arcimboldo Effect: Transformations of the Face from the Sixteenth to the Twentieth Century* (Milan: Bompiani, 1987), 287.

8. Michael Graves, "A Case for Figurative Architecture," in *Michael Graves Buildings and Projects 1966–1981,* ed. Karen Vogel Wheeler, Peter Arnell, and Ted Bickford (New York: Rizzoli, 1982), 11–13.

9. *The Diaries of Paul Klee,* ed. Felix Klee (Los Angeles: University of California Press, 1964), 670.

10. Mies's 1923 talk was delivered in the large lecture hall of the Museum for Applied Arts in Berlin. It was published in *Bauwelt* 14, no. 52, 1923, and republished in English as "Solved Problems: A Demand on Our Building Methods," trans. Rolf Achilles, *Mies van der Rohe: Architect as Educator* (Chicago: University of Chicago Press, 1986), 165–66. Quotations are from this translation.

11. While all architects described in this paragraph are not strictly speaking Modern Movement stock, all, in some way or another, subscribed to Modern Movement tendencies, and all understood architecture not simply as building but as a way of life and a prescription for a good society. In an April 2000 interview, Michael Graves noted what some of these masters and their tendencies toward "total design" had meant to him, explaining his interest in product design by recalling: "When I was growing up in architecture school, my heroes were people like Charles Eames, Le Corbusier, Frank Lloyd Wright, Eero Saarinen, Mies van der Rohe; in other words, without any style inference. All of those people were engaged in production of not only architecture, but of things that would make the character of the room: the furniture, the carpet, the lighting. I always thought that's what architects did." See Rita F. Catinella, "Michael Graves: Man of the House," *Architectural Record,* April 2000, 179.

12. The title of one of Postmodernism's most popular introductions is perhaps worth noting here: Charles Jencks's *The Language of Post-Modern Architecture* (London: Academy Editions, 1977). Page 53 of this book includes color photographs of Graves's neo-Corbu Hanselmann, Benacerraf, and Snyderman houses with captions that note the "syntactic features," "syntactical meaning," and "related syntaxes" of these built metaphors. Page 52 features a photograph of the 1938 "Tail-o-the-pup" Hot Dog Stand in Los Angeles and of the 1976 "Bootmobile," a car disguised as a shoe.

10

The Second Greatest Generation
Michael Sorkin

1. Never Trust Anyone Over . . . ?

For the past twenty years I have been over thirty, the actual milestone having occurred slightly before the lapsing of the seventies (which was when much of the sixties actually occurred). And I am not the only one. As the boomer bulge in the bell curve grinds toward oblivion, we are driven to ask: what has the aging of youth culture meant for architecture?

Youth, of course, is strictly a cultural matter. My generation is by self-definition—the only definition that ever counted for us—young. Architecture, the "old man's profession," has never been congenial to us (among others). We certainly returned the favor: bridling at the "man," many of us rebelled, abandoning architecture, heading for the woods, building by hand, advocating for communities, drawing, making trouble, laying the groundwork for the cultural revolution.

This didn't really work out as we planned. The world seems not to have changed along the lines of the image we had for it. Somehow the "liberating" mantra of sex, drugs, and rock and roll changed into the nightmare of AIDS, Prozac, and MTV. How much of a hand did we have in this cultural devolution?

Burton H. Wolfe, cover of *The Hippies*. Courtesy of The Albert and Shirley Small Special Collections, University of Virginia Library.

2. The Clinton Library

Limiting politics to resistance or selling out has not served us entirely well. Our own first president illustrates the sheer porousness, the corruptibility, of these categories. Clinton is not exactly *one of us*, in the same way that any member of student government during the late sixties was not exactly one of us but rather something between a quisling and a geek (depending on whether one focused on politics or style). Now we are witnessing the spectacle of two co-generationalists running for the presidency. These—the eternal frat boy and the sellout student government type—give the lie to certain fantasies about the triumph of the counterculture. Sixty percent of George W. Bush's class at Yale—the class of '68!—voted for either Richard Nixon or George Wallace. Al Gore elected to go to Vietnam. Patrician universities, with their solid ruling-class values and their various schools of social architecture, have a way of countering countercultural agendas, it seems.

And they have a way of promoting the middle of the road. When the time came for Clinton to choose an architect to design his shrine in Little Rock, did he turn to an architect his own age? Did he seek to radicalize the repository via form or effect? Not at all. He made his choice from the slightly older generation, choosing an architect not quite old enough to be his (absent) father but certainly old enough to Wally his Beaver. The first boomer administration runs from its roots, affecting the same brain-dead Hollywood style that answers the question "Rock and Roll Museum?" with "I. M. Pei" (designer of the first "modern" presidential library). And we haven't heard much lately from the presidential sax, not since Clinton was trying to persuade us that he shared our values (we'll keep our pain to ourselves, thanks).

3. Blah Blah Blah

The political rebellion of the sixties announced itself in the characteristic speech of the late twentieth century: first person. But the self-promoting, self-conscious "I" of my generation has been hobbled by our awareness of the unconscious, which has hovered over us like a specter. This unconscious has not only promised the possibility of a "liberation of desire" from social constraint; it has also rallied skepticism of our best intentions. The unconscious, after all, *always* trumps the conscious as a cause of action and thus of political striving. Beneath the desire to do good lurks a neglected child. Behind the orderliness of minimalism lies crap in the pants. Politics itself has been reduced to just another symptom; it dares not promise a cure for fear of being labeled the dupe of its own neuroses.

Whether this is a proper reading of Freud is really not the issue; it is the reading that undermined our sense of the world's reliability and our own political will, producing a special generational uncertainty principle. We all have our styles of superego, and this combination of license and guilt has distinguished us, on the one hand, from the "greatest generation" of our parents who—dammit—had something unequivocal to fight for, and, on the other, from the Gen X'ers and Y'ers, the Reagan*jugend,* whose traumas seem so *fifties,* inflicted by the pressures of consumption rather than rebellion. Thus, questions of influence acquire for us a special anxiety. The unflagging hegemony of the sixty-something and seventy-something cadre that rules, that formulated the parameters of the depoliticized, desocialized post-modernity that swept architecture in the seventies and eighties, needs a violent shaking from the left.

4. No More Secondhand Dad

What to do when the parents in your own family romance are the stalwarts of the avant-garde? That we received our lessons in artistic rebellion at twice-secondhand somewhat diminished our sense of their originality. Avant-gardism is about rupture, overthrow, the father-murderous rage of art. Classic early-twentieth-century avant-gardism wanted a radical reworking of the visual aspect of architecture *and* a reinvention of the process of production.

The postmodern "avant-garde" is a somewhat different creature. Compromised by a sense of having inherited both its credentials and its topics, its intellectual agenda has remained caught in the avant-garde dream of its ancestors. It thus re-covered much of the ground explored half a century ago, redoubling the received critical discourse with its own metacritical commentary, interpolating another layer of interpretation between the "primary" investigation and its own. The magazine *October,* for example, the bible of postmodernity (and exemplar for our own theorizing), continues to be held hostage by its obsession with surrealism, as with some lost idyll. And architecture carries on with fresh formalisms of the broken (or the perfect) square.

Try as we might, we have not been able to get Oedipus out of our edifices; inherited property still defines us. A false patriarchy continues to structure the discipline and practice of architecture, in which a fraternal order of equals is presided over by a simultaneously dead and obscenely alive father, father Philip, in this instance.

5. Life in the Past Lane

This stalled fascination with former revolutions is the result of a failure of nerve and of invention. It is also evidence of the ideological and psychological trauma that has beset our attempts to formulate an avant-garde in rebellion against an avant-garde to which we desperately desire to remain faithful. The result has been a kind of fission. One by-product is the hyperconservatism of our melancholy historicists. Another is the would-be radicalism that has produced visually novel buildings and rudimentary bridges to the world of the virtual, but that still clings to dusty desires for legitimacy.

The lesson we have been unable to learn is that it takes a lot more rebellion than we have been able to muster to remain faithful to the heritage of the avant-garde.

6. Market Share

I am not sure the *New York Times Magazine* did us any favors with its gossipy, prurient cover story on Rem Koolhaas, our momentary laureate. Depicting him as a kind of edgy Martha Stewart who refuses to judge any endeavor "a good thing," whose mission is the "mission of no mission," the *Times* tried to inscribe his fundamental cynicism into the format of the hero-architect, *Fountainhead*-style. Of course, the paper went for the Hollywood version. Gary Cooper may have behaved like Frank Lloyd Wright, but the models in the background were strictly Gordon Bunshaft.

Sound familiar? The challenge of collapsing the tastemaker and the ideologue is sure to test one side or the other dramatically. Is it possible to be Paul Auster, Sam Walton, and Kim Il Sung at the same time? Will Rem succeed in branding the generic?

7. Africa Shops at Prada

Jetting into Harvard to administer his shopping seminar, Rem snags a job designing Prada stores. The press praises his strategy of branding: no design "identity," instead *a space where things happen,* "an exciting urban environment that creates a unique Prada experience." A TV camera in the dressing room will permit you (TV's *Big Brother* is another Dutch import) to view yourself from all sides at once. Will thousand-dollar shoes move faster when surveilled from all angles? Will there be an algorithm to airbrush away our worst features? Must we buy this privatization of culture? Does the postmodern critique of the museum, the call for tearing down its walls, do anything but free art for the shopping mall? I'll take Bilbao, thanks.

The trouble with an age of scholasticism is that you can talk yourself into the idea that *anything* is politics. By the time it has devolved from direct action to propaganda to critical theory, to the appropriation of theory, to the ironic appropriation of theory, to the branding of theory, to the rejection of theory, something is lost. Critique stokes its own fantasy of participation. On the one hand, this produces boutique design as social practice, and, on the other, it segues into the more rarefied reaches of recombination. My Russian partner, Andrei, has been smoking cheap cigarettes that someone brought him from back home. The bright red pack is emblazoned with a picture of Lenin in high-sixties graphic style. The maker is "Prima," the brand "Nostalgia," the smell appalling. What's next? Lenin Lites and Trotsky 100s? Must we succumb to the speed of this? Can't we slow the whole thing down?

8. Nostalgie de la Boue

This new nostalgia (the nostalgia for packaged nostalgia) is everywhere. Now that my generation rules the media, part of us keep busy looting our experience for the rudest forms of exploitation. If you have turned on your TV lately, you might have seen *That '70s Show,* a slick package of affects, the decade as a set of tics and styles. The expropriation continues to the limits of corporate memory. Advertising nowadays is lush with sixties themes as fiftyish account executives preside over the wholesale trashing of the culture that nourished them. "I Feel Good"— a laxative. "Forever Young"—invidious irony—incontinence diapers.

On *Survivor,* flaming torches turn the game-show paradise island into Trader Vic's.

Nostalgic for fifties and sixties styles, yet too hip not to be troubled by the accumulated political baggage of the project, this cadre of media masters offers a stance of almost pure cynicism. "I am saying this, but I don't actually believe it; in fact, I don't actually believe anything, because it is no longer possible to do so." With Niemayer or Lapidus or Harrison as the soundtrack (and the Stones, perhaps, playing on the answering machine), they seem to want to suspend indefinitely the moment when they would be obliged to take a position.

A microgenerational conflict now exists among those for whom the sixties represents a source of anxiety, those for whom the decade still represents possibility, and those for whom it is simply ancient history. Most invested in the middle alternative, I grapple with this legacy, but the particulars grow vague (the feeling stays evergreen).

9. That Vision Thing

Our fantasies did have vision, the product, mainly, of the working out of certain congruent themes of prior modernisms. Those domes and inflatables and garbage housing were not just technologically and environmentally prescient; they also figured—whether in civil rights or Woodstock variants—in political ideas about the extension, openness, and spontaneity of spaces of assembly. And the canny melding of technological control with an "anti"-technological ideology gave birth to appropriate technology.

The alternative visuality of the sixties, however, has had only the most marginal impact on architecture. (Many breathe a sigh of relief.) The psychedelic style that included Fillmore posters, the Merry Pranksters bus, and Sgt. Pepperesque couture required a certain lag before becoming appropriatable by architecture. We liberated the seventies supreme soviet—Venturi, Stern, Moore, Graves, et al.—from the kitsch closet and made it permissible for them to love Vegas and the roadside. But always they had to rationalize their love, to capture it for their outmoded agendas and fantasies of control. We responded with disengagement and irony, as usual.

The "appropriated" art of so many artists of my generation was a typically limp response, immediately gobbled up by the art machine. Having bought into a critical history that denigrated intentions, we then bought into our own ironical reappropriation of intentionality via obsessive proceduralisms and poetic trances. Too late! Narcissism is not the same as self-confidence. Even *Seinfeld* has been cancelled.

10. Vive la Différence!

The Whole Earth Catalog and *Our Bodies, Ourselves* are our holy books, good news for a political body and a contested environment both. These really were milestones: we are all a little more gay now, a little closer to the earth, a little more skeptical about the system's "choices." The politicization of the personal (as the formula *should* have been) demands idiosyncrasy beyond the tonsorial and sartorial. Pity about our architecture. So many interesting sites wasted.

11. It Isn't Easy Being Green

We always hear that green architecture "looks bad," and most of it does. At the end of the day, though, separating your trash is probably a greater contribution to world architecture than Bilbao.

Well, maybe not Bilbao.

2000

Contributors

Michael Benedikt is Hal Box Chair in Urbanism and director of the Center for American Architecture and Design at the University of Texas at Austin. His books include *Deconstructing the Kimbell* and *For an Architecture of Reality*, and he is editor of the book series CENTER.

Luis Fernández-Galiano is editor of *Arquitectura Viva* and author of *Fire and Memory: On Architecture and Energy*.

Kenneth Frampton is Ware Professor of Architecture at Columbia University. His books include *Labour, Work, and Architecture: Collected Essays on Architecture and Design* and *Le Corbusier: Architect of the Twentieth Century*.

Thomas Frank is author of *What's the Matter with Kansas? How Conservatives Won the Heart of America* and *One Market under God: Extreme Capitalism, Market Populism, and the End of Economic Democracy*. He is coeditor of *The Baffler*.

Kevin Ervin Kelley is co-owner of Shook Kelley in Los Angeles and Charlotte, North Carolina. He lectures in executive education seminars at the Harvard University Graduate School of Design with a focus on leveraging consumer perceptions.

Daniel Naegele is an architect, critic, and assistant professor of architecture at Iowa State University.

Rick Poynor writes about design, media, and visual culture. He is the author of *Design without Boundaries* and *Obey the Giant: Life in the Image World.*

William S. Saunders is editor of *Harvard Design Magazine.* His books include *Modern Architecture: Photographs of Ezra Stoller.*

Michael Sorkin is the principal of the Michael Sorkin Studio in New York City and director of the graduate program in urban design at the City College of New York. His most recent books include *Some Assembly Required* (Minnesota, 2001), *The Next Jerusalem: Sharing the Divided City,* and *Starting from Zero: Reconstructing Downtown New York.*

Wouter Vanstiphout is an architectural historian and one of the founders of the Rotterdam research and design firm Crimson. He is coeditor of *Mart Stam's Trousers* and *Too Blessed to Be Depressed,* and coauthor of *Profession Architect: De Architekten Cie.*